FAST FOOD
FOR SUSTAINED
ENERGY

Optimal, not perfect nutrition

ACKNOWLEDGEMENTS

A great big thank you to our families for their patience while we obsessed and laboured over the databases that make up the backbone of the practical advice given in these pages.

A heartfelt word of thanks also to Christine Stent Pinha, our esteemed colleague, who was part of the initial concept and development of this book.

Thank you to our editor, Vanessa Vineall, and to photographer Berna Coetzee and food stylist Sonja Jordt for the excellent photos that make this book so user friendly.

Last, but not least, our thanks to our publisher, Ansie Kamffer, for her faith in this project.

First published in 2011
Tafelberg, An imprint of NB Publishers,
a division of Media24 Boeke (Pty) Ltd ,
40 Heerengracht, Cape Town 8001

Fourth impression 2013

Editorial assistant: Lindy Samery
Editor: Vanessa Vineall
Design: Anton Sassenberg
Typesetting: Wim Reinders
Index: Anna Tanneberger
Photographer: Berna Coetzee
Styling: Sonja Jordt
Make-up artist: Mariaan Enslin
Props: Maia du Plessis

FSC
www.fsc.org
MIX
Paper from
responsible sources
FSC® C105735 Printed in South Africa by Interpak Books

ISBN: 978-0-624-05266-1
ISBN: 978-0-624-05840-3 (epub)

FAST FOOD FOR SUSTAINED ENERGY

Optimal, not perfect nutrition

GABI STEENKAMP *RD(SA)*
& CELYNN ERASMUS *RD(SA)*
Registered Dieticians SA

TAFELBERG

CONTENTS

Halloumi cheese on toast. (Recipe on page 62.)

WHAT THIS BOOK IS ALL ABOUT

Rushing around with more things to get done than there are hours in a day seems to be the norm for many of us today. Family and work commitments, social pressures and the daily challenges of a full life tend to make health and nutrition less of a pressing concern. It is no wonder that we resort to using ready-made foods for refuelling, and as much as we believe good nutrition and health should be a priority, without the nutrition knowledge and skills this seems an insurmountable challenge that we shelve for another week, another month, another year.

This book is not about perfect nutrition, but rather an attempt to address the reality that many people do not have the time or inclination to eat perfectly, but would be happy to make an effort if good nutrition could be easily accomplished within the context of their lives. This book helps to make nutrition an easily attainable priority on a daily basis. Bite-sized nutrition facts partnered with the practical skills to optimise the use of ready-made foods, dishes and meals make it easy to get a grip on good nutrition.

Regular balanced meals are necessary to maintain stable blood glucose levels to optimise concentration and sustained energy, and are easily put together from basic ingredients as shown in the meal sections. The emphasis is on swift preparation where meals are assembled and not cooked.

Takeaways such as pizza and hamburgers can be the basis of a reasonably balanced meal as long as the portion is adjusted and the missing colour from nature's colour palette is added.

Smart snacking is an integral part of eating on the run and this book includes plenty of such suggestions. For those who want to stock up on healthy home-made snacks, it includes a few quick and useful recipes – biscotti, bran muffins and ginger biscuits. And for those who have to buy their meals or snacks, the Appendix includes handy checklists.

The Portion Distortion and Build-a-meal sections are a fun way to learn just how the food industry has hoodwinked us into eating more than we need, one of the reasons for the worldwide increase in waistlines and poor health. That simple movie snack and drink combo could in fact be the same as eating a full day's food intake in one sitting.

With all this food information, you will be able to make better choices and meal combinations so that good nutrition can once again be an easily achievable goal.

YOUR NUTRITION ASSESSMENT

Fill in this assessment of your eating habits to find out how you fare.
Tick the boxes next to those statements that apply to you. If you eat the indicated food or adhere to the principle four days a week or less, do not tick the box. Only tick the box if the food or principle applies to you five or more days per week.

HOW WELL DO YOU EAT?

☐ I eat a balanced breakfast at least five days a week.

☐ I eat breakfast, lunch and supper at least five days a week, or small snacks throughout the day because I do not have time for meals.

☐ I eat a minimum of two tennis-ball-sized portions of fresh fruit at least five days a week.

☐ I eat at least three tennis ball-sized portions of vegetables or salad at least five days a week.

☐ I choose lower fat food options 80% of the time – lower fat cheese, milk and yoghurt; lean meat, ostrich and venison; grilled, not fried foods; low-oil dressings and mayonnaise; and so on.

☐ My meat, fish or chicken portions are no bigger than the palm of my hand 80% of the time, even when eating out.

☐ I include a small serving of nuts, seeds, avocado, olives or nut butters at least three days a week, as snacks or in foods such as seeds and nuts in muesli, avocado on toast, or olives in salad.

☐ When using fat in cooking or preparing food, I use small amounts of the healthier oils 80% of the time – olive oil, canola oil, palm fruit oil, avocado oil.

☐ I eat some omega-3-rich food at least five times a week – fresh or smoked salmon, pilchards, sardines, other fatty fish, omega-3-rich eggs, flax seeds, linseeds, linseed oil, flax oil.

☐ I understand and use the glycemic index (GI) when making food choices most of the time.

☐ I understand and consider the glycemic load (GL) of foods when choosing my serving sizes.

☐ When buying meals, snacks or beverages, I choose the smallest portion 80% of the time.

☐ I make sure I drink enough water every day; that is my body weight in kilograms divided by 10 to give the number of glasses of water I should drink per day (one glass = 200 ml minimum).

☐ I limit my daily caffeine intake to no more than three cups of coffee or three single espressos or six cups of regular tea or two energy drinks or three hot chocolates, or three cola drinks.

☐ I limit my alcohol intake to none at all, or one or two units per day – one single tot, 125 ml wine, 330 ml beer.

HOW MANY TICKS DID YOU GET?

10-15: A score of 10-15 indicates that you are convinced that good nutrition is important and that is has become part of your lifestyle.

5-10: This score shows that you are aware of the basics of good nutrition. However, your modern lifestyle or lack of knowledge or motivation may be interfering with your ability to put good nutrition principles into practice.

0-5: A score of less than five indicates that nutrition is not your priority and that you may be lacking the knowledge or tools to properly implement good eating habits.

With this book you will not only have plenty of food for thought that is easy to digest, but you will also gain the skills to put optimised nutrition into practice.

one
LIFESTYLE CHALLENGES OF EATING ON THE RUN

With all the rushing around and juggling of family, work and social commitments, lifestyle challenges can get in the way of good nutrition. Such challenges include daily stresses and lack of time with the resultant despondent mindset, forgetting to drink enough water, obligatory travel and easy access to unhealthy foods.

The guidelines that follow will help you to better manage these lifestyle challenges of eating on the run so that you can sustain your energy levels, work smarter and get more out of your day.

The smarter choice is to eat half a tramezzini with a large salad.

VENDING MACHINES, OFFICE TROLLEYS AND TUCK SHOPS

Most of the foods on offer are high in saturated and total fat, sodium and/or sugar, and virtually devoid of fibre and vitamins. Eating these foods on a regular basis may result in erratic blood sugar levels, leaving you with low energy, irritability, poor concentration, weight gain and an increased risk of diabetes, heart attacks and stroke, gout, high blood pressure, cancer, and other diseases.

MANAGING THIS CHALLENGE

- ☐ Before grabbing a snack, consider whether you rather need a break from what you're doing. Going for a short walk or getting a breath of fresh air may be all you need to feel re-energized.

- ☐ Before having a snack, drink a glass of water as you may simply be dehydrated.

- ☐ Think before you buy a snack. Often just seeing tempting snacks will stimulate appetite but not actual hunger.

- ☐ Do not allow yourself to become very hungry by missing meals. Hungry people tend to make unhealthy food choices, particularly if tempting snacks are readily available.

- ☐ If you must have that bar of chocolate or packet of crisps, choose the smallest size and consider sharing your snack with a colleague or friend.

- ☐ When choosing a beverage, preferably choose water or opt for a sugar-free cold drink rather than a sugar-laden cold drink.

- ☐ Ask for healthier snacks to be provided. For ideas, see the Smart Snacking section on pages 77 to 78.

- ☐ Your best option is to have your own supply of smart snacks. Refer to the Smart Snacking section on page 72 for how to read snack labels and a list of smart snack ideas.

CAFFEINE-RICH DRINKS

Overconsumption of caffeine often goes hand in hand with overconsumption of sugar and refined unhealthy snacks such as biscuits. Excess caffeine intake may cause feelings of anxiety, increased blood pressure, insomnia and headaches. It can also be a digestive system irritant, causing heartburn, cramping or diarrhoea in sensitive individuals.

MANAGING THIS CHALLENGE

☐ Before having a cup of tea or coffee, consider whether you do not simply need a break. A short walk or a breath of fresh air may be all you need.

☐ Coffee, regular tea, hot chocolate, cola drinks and some energy drinks contain caffeine. Coffee and tea should be limited to three cups per day and hot chocolate, cola drinks and energy drinks should not be consumed on a regular basis, but rather as a treat.

☐ Avoid coffee and tea creamers, as they are high in saturated and trans fats, which increase the risk of diabetes, cancer, heart attacks and stroke.

☐ The total daily sugar intake for an adult should be less than 10% of total energy, which equates to eight teaspoons of sugar per day for women, and 12 teaspoons for men.

☐ Although tea, coffee and cocoa contain beneficial flavonoids and other antioxidants, the caffeine content limits their benefit.

☐ With every cup of coffee or tea, drink a glass of water to quench your thirst. In winter, drink hot water with a slice of lemon, orange or fresh ginger in it. Herbal teas also count as water.

☐ To cut back on caffeine, choose decaffeinated coffee. If you are not a coffee lover, you may enjoy a natural coffee substitute such as chicory.

☐ Refer to the Portion Distortion section on beverages on page 134.

INADEQUATE WATER INTAKE

Most beverages on offer when you're on the run are not pure water, making it difficult to ensure proper hydration. Even mild dehydration may result in reduced concentration capacity, false hunger, headaches, joint pain, poor digestion and lower energy levels.

MANAGING THIS CHALLENGE

☐ A good estimate of how much water you should drink per day is to take your body weight in kilograms and divide it by 10, giving you the number of glasses of water you need per day. For example, a 60 kg woman would need about six glasses of water per day. One glass of water is a minimum of 200 ml.

☐ Start your day with a glass of hot water. For extra zing, add lemon slices, fresh ginger or mint.

☐ Fruit-infused water that is available all day makes for a delicious thirst quencher.

☐ Keep water with you at all times: a jug or bottle of water on your desk and at all meetings, bottled water in your car and filtered water in the kitchen. In summer, freeze water overnight and enjoy ice cold throughout the day. In short, keep water visible so that you actually drink it.

☐ Herbal teas, hot or chilled, make a delicious source of water.

☐ Every cup of regular tea or coffee should be accompanied by a glass of water.

☐ Water can be flavoured with artificially sweetened cordials, but keep to no more than one litre of flavoured water per day.

☐ When you think you are hungry, have a glass of water first as you may simply be thirsty. Thirst should be quenched with water and not juices and soft drinks.

MEETINGS

The challenge with meetings is that either unhealthy foods are provided or none at all. Foods on offer during meetings such as pies, biscuits, sausage rolls, samoosas, spring rolls and sandwiches are highly refined and high in fat. This can limit engagement and creativity and promote weight gain.

MANAGING THIS CHALLENGE

☐ Be proactive and if possible, organise healthy food platters for meetings. See the photographs over the page and the Smart Snacking section on pages 77 and 78 for ideas. There are also various catering outlets that provide delicious smart snack platters.

☐ Suggested snack platter items: cucumber strips, mini spring onions, falafels, baby carrots, mini pitas, dried apricots, asparagus spears, cherry tomatoes, tzatziki, hummus and low-fat cottage cheese as a dip, mini meatballs, olives, celery sticks, mini mozzarella balls, berries, boiled eggs, chicken strips, dried mango, Peppadews, shaved cold meat, grapes, snap peas, baby corn, pineapple, sweet peppers, smoked salmon, crackers/Provitas, etc.

☐ Keep your own healthy snacks on hand to consume during or between back-to-back meetings.

☐ Ensure that water is available in all meetings along with the tea and coffee.

☐ Meetings are best scheduled between meals, rather than at meal times. Rather have a smart snack before meetings and then a beverage during the meeting.

☐ If you have to eat from unhealthy food platters, rather fill a plate of food once, keeping in mind that half should be vegetables or fruit. In this way, you end up eating a fairly balanced meal rather than too many high fat, high carbohydrate snacks if you nibble continuously.

☐ If there are four or fewer of you who need to have a meeting, consider going for a walk while addressing the issues at hand. This helps to reduce unhealthy snacking.

Suggested snack platter for meetings (overleaf).

EATING AWAY FROM HOME

Eating out and takeaway meals increase the temptation to over-indulge, have treats and consume unbalanced meals, resulting in difficult weight management, increased lifestyle disease risk and poor energy management.

MANAGING THIS CHALLENGE

☐ No matter where you are eating, remember to fill half of your plate with colour from nature's colour palette: salad or vegetables. The meat, fish or chicken portion should be about the size of the palm of your hand, and the starch (including the bread and pudding) should be the size of your fist.

☐ Hot chips, a regular item on restaurant and takeaway menus, are high in unhealthy fats and kilojoules and are not needed as part of a meal. See the Portion Distortion section on page 92 for more information.

☐ Salad is a healthy choice as long as the dressing is low in fat. A salad should not be drowned in dressing – only drizzle on enough to enhance the flavours of the salad. Remember that salads with protein (chicken, tuna, salmon, cheese, and so on) are a meal in themselves.

☐ Meat and vegetable sauces can also be high in fat. Order them on the side and only drizzle the sauce over the food.

☐ Dishes with the sauce already plated are acceptable as long as you eat the vegetable or protein with just enough sauce to add depth of flavour and leave most of the sauce on the plate.

☐ Eat regular meals so that it is easier to make wise food choices when eating away from home. If necessary, have a smart snack such as fresh fruit, low-fat yoghurt or a handful of nuts before eating out.

☐ Eat mindfully. Be aware of the textures and flavour sensations of the food you are eating. Savour every mouthful, and eat slowly. Remember that it takes 10 to 20 minutes for the "feel full" message to register in your brain.

☐ Fruit juices, soft drinks, milkshakes, smoothies, energy drinks and alcoholic beverages are strictly speaking too energy dense to have with meals. You should rather make water your beverage of choice with all meals. Alcohol on an empty stomach is also not recommended.

☐ Vegetarian dishes are not necessarily a healthier option, as they can be very high in fat due to the cheese, fried items and cream.

☐ Omit the starch (bread, potato, chips, pasta) from your main meal if you choose to have a starter or a pudding.

☐ Restaurant and takeaway portions are generally too big. Keep to a fistful of starch, protein the size of the palm of your hand and generous helpings of vegetables and salad. If possible order half or starter portions, and if this is not an option, take the excess food home and refrigerate within two hours. Alternatively, keep a frozen ice brick in a small cooler bag in your car and refrigerate the leftovers as soon as possible.

☐ If you are easily tempted by the sight of delicious food, avoid buffets.

☐ It helps to decide on what you would like to eat before getting to a restaurant to avoid the temptation of ordering less healthy items while distracted by others around you.

☐ Avoid the bread or rolls that are offered as you are seated, unless you would prefer to eat the bread in place of the starch at your meal.

☐ Be careful of dessert denial, as it can be counterproductive. Most people feel that dessert rounds off a good meal. However, desserts are high in fat and kilojoules. Rather share a dessert between two to four people to satisfy the need for a sweet ending. Alternatively, opt for a sweet decaffeinated skinny cappuccino.

☐ For advice on managing the challenge of takeaway items such as pizza, hamburgers, fried chicken, wraps and so on, see the Portion Distortion section on page 82.

TRAVELLING

Whether you spend a lot of time in a car or hotels, or fly across time zones, travelling disrupts your usual eating routine and can play havoc with healthier food choices.

MANAGING THIS CHALLENGE

☐ The biggest challenge with meals served on aeroplanes is the almost complete lack of vegetables and fresh fruit. Make sure you do eat all the salad and vegetables that are served, and then limit the starch of the meal to a maximum of two choices of either the bread roll, pastry, crisps, chocolate, cake, biscuits, pudding, or cooked starch.

☐ Should you wish to have a meal before boarding a plane, choose a salad-based meal with a small protein serving.

☐ Meal timing is the other challenge when travelling. A main meal should only be consumed four to five hours after the last main meal. Should you be served a meal one to two hours after a large meal, treat this meal as a snack, rather than consuming the whole meal.

☐ If possible, carry a good selection of smart snacks with you. See the Smart Snacking section on page 77.

☐ Fruit juices, soft drinks and alcoholic beverages are strictly speaking too energy dense to have with meals. Rather make water your beverage of choice with all meals. Alcohol on an empty stomach is not recommended, and be sure to match every alcoholic drink with a full glass of water.

☐ Drinking enough water is very important, as long flights are particularly dehydrating. Have a glass of water every hour or so.

☐ If you spend lots of time travelling, see the sections on Breakfasts on page 29, Lunches and Dinners on page 47, Portion Distortion on page 81, and the previous section on managing the challenges of eating away from home.

LACK OF TIME

Not having enough time is everybody's reality and is often the reason why nutrition is compromised and no longer a priority.

MANAGING THIS CHALLENGE

- ☐ Modern food availability distorts the natural choice of healthy foods. That is why correct nutrition knowledge and skills are essential for better food choices. This book provides these.

- ☐ A well-stocked kitchen with the correct foods makes it so much easier to assemble balanced meals in a jiffy and to eat healthily on the run. Keep a small notebook and a pen in the kitchen so that you can add foods to your shopping list as you use them up. Ordering online is also a convenient option.

- ☐ Free time on weekends can be used to prepare or bake meals and snacks ahead of time.

- ☐ Make use of recipe books that offer quick, healthy meals. Try the *Eating for Sustained Energy* range by Gabi Steenkamp and Liesbet Delport Tafelberg), and *Simply Good Food* by Justine Drake (Lannice Snyman Publishers). Choose one or two recipes and compile a shopping list so that you have all the ingredients available when you want to make these dishes.

- ☐ For advice on cooking ahead and more time-saving tips, see the sections on Breakfasts, and Lunches and Dinners on pages 29 and 47.

- ☐ On occasion you may wish to use caterers who provide healthier ready-cooked meals.

UNHEALTHY FOOD RELATIONSHIP

A healthy relationship with food is manifested in the enjoyment of food flavours and textures balanced with an appreciation of the physiological function of food and eating in response to real hunger, and not appetite. Aberrant food relationships occur when there is obsessive behaviour linked to food intake, which can manifest as overeating, under-eating, or fanaticism about any particular food(s).

MANAGING THIS CHALLENGE

☐ Enjoyment of eating is important, but so too is being able to distinguish between living to eat and eating to live.

☐ Health fanaticism can be detrimental to your health by causing nutritional deficiencies and encouraging obsessive behaviour. Aim for progress, not perfection. An all-or-nothing approach is counterproductive. Set yourself up for success by making a few small changes and making them part of your lifestyle. Rather than deciding to drink more water and eat more fruit and vegetables, be specific by keeping a glass of water at your desk at all times; deciding to eat fresh fruit as your afternoon snack while you drive home; ordering a salad as a starter when you eat out, and so on.

☐ Eat mindfully. Be aware of the textures and flavour sensations of the food you are eating. Savour every mouthful, and eat slowly. Remember that it takes 10 to 20 minutes for the "feel full" message to register.

☐ Keeping a food diary creates self-awareness and can identify where you are eating too much or too little.

☐ Awareness is the first step to change. Try to identify whether you were rewarded with treats or sweets as a child for good behaviour or mishaps, such as falling off a swing. This may be a reason for emotional eating in adulthood. Rather manage your boredom, loneliness, frustration, and mishaps with non-food-related activities such as reading a book or favourite magazine, calling a friend, spending time in nature, walking or perhaps writing in your journal.

☐ Be aware that there is a difference between hunger and emotional eating. Before eating, ask yourself, "Am I really hungry or am I responding to other hunger triggers?" Hunger triggers include the delicious aroma or sight of food, emotions, traditional meal times, and so on.

☐ Thirst is often perceived as hunger, so drink a glass of water before responding to your apparent hunger.

☐ Denying yourself the foods you love will most probably result in cravings and bingeing. Be balanced and allow yourself to have guilt-free treats. Healthy enjoyment of food is characterised by good portion control.

☐ Movement such as a brisk walk or workout releases the same "feel-good" brain chemicals that are released when eating. Laughter will also release these endorphins.

☐ Regular check-ups can be a wake-up call to health problems such as being over- or underweight, high cholesterol, high blood pressure, diabetes and pre-diabetes.

two BREAKFASTS

You've heard it before: breakfast is the most important meal of the day. Miss breakfast and you'll need to make up an additional quarter (25%) of your daily nutrient needs, and we are not talking about calories or kilojoules!

Breakfast is vital to starting your day on a firm footing and getting the competitive edge. Eating a nutritious, balanced breakfast within two hours or so of waking will:

☐ Provide you with sustained energy and enhanced mental performance.

☐ Help you experience fewer food cravings.

☐ Raise your metabolism significantly, assisting with weight loss and weight management.

Grab-and-go breakfast options. (Details on page 38.)

What's holding you back from a sunny-side-up start to the day? Why do you miss out on this all-important meal? Have a look at some of the reasons why you may be missing out, then take note of at least one of the practical strategies we have used ourselves so that we remain at our best for most of the day.

☐ There's just no time!

Most of the breakfast ideas below require only a minute or two to prepare. Making a smoothie, for example, can take less than two minutes and it can easily be consumed in the car while driving to work.

☐ I'm not hungry

If you constantly wake up and get going without eating, you will train your body not to be hungry. Rather opt for something light and easy such as a small fruit smoothie or even just a piece of fruit. Do this on a regular basis and you will find your morning appetite reappearing, reminding you to have the most important meal of the day.

☐ I am nauseous in the early morning

It is not necessary to eat as soon as you get up. As long as your breakfast is eaten within two hours of waking, your body will be getting the fuel it needs to optimise functioning on all levels.

☐ When I eat breakfast I am constantly hungry

This is common in our modern times of highly refined breakfast foods. The secret is to choose those foods that are absorbed slowly and steadily throughout the morning, rather than the refined, fast-release cereals so readily available. Always ensure there is some protein in your breakfast. It helps to balance blood sugar levels and to keep you energised for longer. A healthy appetite is a good sign – it usually means your metabolism is increasing, and the correct response is to eat small regular meals throughout the day, starting with a delicious quick breakfast.

☐ Eating breakfast will make me gain weight

In fact, the opposite is true: breakfast can help with weight loss. After a night's sleep, the body needs food to "break" the overnight "fast" and kick-start the metabolism. This increase in metabolism can assist with weight control. Breakfast-eaters also experience fewer food cravings, enabling them to make smarter food and portion choices throughout the day.

BALANCED BREAKFASTS

Step 1 Half-fill your plate with colour from nature's colour palette in the form of fruit or vegetables such as grilled tomatoes, mushrooms, roasted vegetables, and so on.

Step 2 Choose one fistful of starch in the form of low-GI toast, high-fibre cereal, baked beans, and so on.

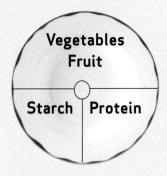

Step 3 Choose a portion (the size of the palm of your hand) of low-fat dairy or lean protein, such as low-fat yoghurt, cheese, egg, fish, and so on.

Step 4 Have a small portion of healthy fat, such as nuts, seeds, peanut butter or avocado. Alternatively, a small amount of good quality oil could be used to prepare the breakfast.

The balanced breakfast ideas in this chapter give amounts for women. Men would consume 1½ times the amounts given. Each breakfast (women's portion) provides:
- [ ] less than 1 500 kilojoules (360 calories)
- [ ] less than 10 g fat
- [ ] less than 45 g carbohydrate
- [ ] a GL around 20
- [ ] as much fibre as possible.

FIBRE-BOOST BREAKFAST

(pictured)

1 Pour ¾ c high-fibre cereal (High Fibre, All Bran Flakes) into a serving bowl.
2 Add ½ c fat-free/skimmed milk.
3 Add lots of fresh berries.
4 Sprinkle with 10 almonds (10 g).
5 Serve with a tiny glass of fresh fruit juice (100 ml) and a large glass of water.

Food facts Consumption of high-fibre foods requires extra water. Using All Bran Flakes the GL is 29, which is a bit high, but the breakfast is still balanced. Using Hi Fibre the GL is 22 and it contains 50% more fibre (15 g). (For more about the glycemic load and why it is important, turn to page 74.)

OATS WITH CINNAMON APPLE

1 Mix 5 T raw oats with ½ c fat-free/skimmed milk.
2 Add 1 large chopped or grated apple.
3 Top with cinnamon, a dash of vanilla essence and 1 T sunflower seeds.

Variation For a Bircher-type muesli, mix all the ingredients the night before and refrigerate.

BERRY MUESLI

1 Top 1 small tub of low-fat plain yoghurt (125 ml or 100 ml) with 5 T low-fat, low-GI muesli (with dried fruit, unsalted nuts and seeds in the muesli).
2 Enjoy with a tiny glass of berry juice (100 ml) to complement the sweet muesli.

FILLED PAPINO

1 Fill half a medium papino (small variety of pawpaw) with $\frac{1}{3}$ c fat-free vanilla yoghurt.
2 Top with 3 T low-GI muesli and 6 chopped pecan nut halves.

FRUITY INSTANT PORRIDGE

1 Spoon 5 T whole-wheat Pronutro (Apple Bake or Original flavour) into a bowl.
2 Pour over 150 ml fat-free/skimmed milk.
3 Add 1 small sliced banana or 1 large pear, chopped.
4 Top with 10 cashew nuts.

Fibre-boost breakfast.

SALMON ON RYE

1 Spread 1 slice seed loaf or rye bread with 3 T smooth fat-free cottage cheese (flavoured).
2 Arrange 2 thin slices smoked salmon on top.
3 Serve with 1 fresh apple cut into wedges and lots of sliced strawberries.

Food facts This breakfast provides 1 100 mg omega-3 essential fats per portion, which equates to a full day's requirement. Omega-3s are essential for brain function, cardiac health and reducing the body's allergic responses. Seed loaf has roughly double the fibre of regular brown bread and is therefore the healthier choice.

FRUITY COTTAGE CHEESE

1 Mix 6 T low-fat cottage cheese, 1 heaped T sultanas, 1 T sunflower seeds and 4 chopped dried apricot halves.
2 Spread generously onto 1 slice rye or seed loaf toast.

Tip One tub of cottage cheese with triple the ingredients above makes three times the amount of this topping. Store the rest in the fridge and use as a filling for mini pita pockets, or spread on crackers or toast.

Food fact Cottage cheese is a good source of low-fat protein but does not count as a source of calcium.

PEANUT BUTTER AND APPLE GRILL

1 Heat the grill.
2 Spread 1 T peanut butter onto 1 slice seed loaf.
3 Top with 2 thinly sliced apple quarters.
4 Drizzle with 1 level t runny honey.
5 Grill for a few moments until browned.
6 Enjoy the other apple half while grilling the meal.

Food fact Honey is twice as concentrated as sugar, so use tiny amounts.

BEANS ON TOAST

1 Warm 3 heaped T baked beans.
2 Spoon onto 1 slice toasted low-GI or rye bread.
3 Top with 2 T grated low-fat cheese.
4 Serve with ½ cup fresh fruit salad.

Food fact Thanks to the baked beans, this breakfast provides 12 g fibre, which is more than double the fibre of most breakfasts.

SAVOURY MINCE ON TOAST

1 Warm 4 T leftover savoury mince mixed with 1 heaped T baked beans.
2 Place 2 thick slices fresh tomato on 1 slice toasted low-GI or rye bread.
3 Spoon the warm savoury mince on top.
4 Serve with 1 fresh fruit of choice.

POACHED EGG

(pictured)

1 Heat 1 t olive oil with 1 t balsamic vinegar in a frying pan.
2 Add 10 cherry tomatoes and cook until they start bursting.
3 Poach 1 egg while the tomatoes cook.
4 Spoon the tomatoes onto 1 slice rye or seed loaf toast and top with the poached egg.
5 Sprinkle generously with fresh parsley or herbs.
6 Serve with a tiny glass of pure fruit juice (100 ml).

Food facts The easiest way to poach eggs is to invest in a microwave egg poacher.
If you prefer, you can replace the poached egg with a boiled one. Because 100 ml fruit juice is so little, add as much chilled water as you like to make a fuller glass of diluted fruit juice.

FRITTATA

1 Spray a frying pan with non-stick cooking spray.
2 Stir-fry ½ sweet pepper with ½ cup mushrooms.
3 Pour over 2 beaten eggs and cook until set to make a frittata.
4 Sprinkle with fresh or dried herbs.
5 Serve the frittata on 1 slice toasted low-GI bread.

Food fact To balance this meal, make sure your mid-morning snack is a fresh fruit.

Poached egg.

GRAB-AND-GO 1
(Pictured on page 28)
Grab 6 dried mango strips and add
2 matchboxes camembert or brie
cheese. Add a bottle of water.

Food fact Fruit and cheese make a
balanced meal. The cheese provides the protein and fat of the
meal, and the fruit supplies the
carbohydrate.

GRAB-AND-GO 2
(Pictured on page 28)
One 40 g "health" bar (see Smart
Snacking section on page 72).
Add 1 small handful of lean biltong
and 6 dried apple rings or soft
eating dried apricots. Plus a bottle
of water.

Food fact Because biltong is so
concentrated this small amount
of biltong provides two meat
portions.

GRAB-AND-GO 3
(Pictured on page 28)
350 ml fat-free or low-fat drinking
yoghurt or milk (flavoured) plus
10 almonds.

Food facts Drinking yoghurt
contains concentrated carbohydrates of which 30 g (6 t) is sugar.
Adding almonds, rather than
more carbohydrate in the form of
fruit, gives a better meal balance.
If you have the time, it would be
better to make a fruit smoothie
(recipes from page 40).

SMOOTHIES

Smoothies are a great meal on the run. Although they are quick and easy to make, the trick is to get the nutrient and energy balance right. The biggest problem with smoothies is that they can be too concentrated, and too big. This means that the glycemic load (GL) is often double what it should be.

Smoothies need to be consumed as soon as possible so drink immediately or pour into a water bottle to drink on the run. Keep the blender within easy reach on the counter top, not packed in the cupboard and definitely not in the box! Adding ice cubes is a great way to add volume without additional kilo-joules. If your smoothie is too thick, simply add water.

Making balanced, healthy smoothies

Step 1 Use no more than two tennis balls of fresh fruit per person. Peel fruit only when necessary, for example in the case of citrus fruits, banana or pine-apple. Chopped fruit and berries can be frozen for easy year-round availabil-ity and convenience. Fruit juice should generally not be added to smoothies, as it is too concentrated.

Step 2 The fruit and the yoghurt provide enough carbohydrate and therefore it is not necessary to add a starch. If you prefer to have extra fibre in your smoothie, add 2-3 T oats, oat bran or digestive bran.

Step 3 Add low-fat or fat-free yoghurt or milk, protein powder or egg to pro-vide the protein.

Step 4 A small portion of healthy fat, such as nuts, seeds, peanut butter, avo-cado, or oil (macadamia, avocado or omega oil) can be added if the protein used is fat free.

Here are some balanced smoothie ideas, with the amounts listed for women. Men could consume 1½ times to twice the amounts given.

Each smoothie below (women's portion size) provides:
- [ ] less than 1 200 kilojoules (290 calories)
- [ ] less than 10 g fat
- [ ] less than 55 g carbohydrate
- [ ] 7-12 g protein
- [ ] at least 4 g fibre
- [ ] a GL around 20.

TROPICAL MORNING
(pictured)
½ medium pawpaw, peeled and pips removed (150 g)
1 kiwi fruit, peeled (65 g)
50 ml fruit juice (3 T)
14 cashew nuts, raw (20 g)
30 ml protein powder
200 ml water
ice cubes (optional)

Place all the ingredients in a blender and blend until smooth.

Food fact This is a dairy-free smoothie provided that a milk-free protein powder is used. There is no need to add lots of protein powder, as a breakfast need only provide 7-14 g protein.

PEAR-FECTION
1 large or 2 small pears (220 g)
1 handful white grapes (75 g)
5 T low-fat vanilla yoghurt (75 ml)
¼ c water (60 ml)
1½ t oat bran (7.5 ml)
7 almonds, raw (10 g)
ice cubes (optional)

Place all the ingredients in a blender and blend until smooth.

Food fact This smoothie has the lowest GI of the six recipes given, despite the grapes in it.

PEANUT POWER
1 small apple (75 g)
2 T low-GI muesli (30 g)
6 T fat-free/skimmed milk (90 ml)
5 T fat-free vanilla yoghurt (75 ml)
1 rounded t peanut butter (10 g)
ice cubes (optional)

Place all the ingredients in a blender and blend until smooth.

Food fact Fat-free milk and yoghurt are recommended because the peanut butter contributes the fat.

Tropical morning smoothie.

BERRY-LICIOUS

(pictured)

1 c frozen or fresh berries (125 g)

1 large banana (150 g)

1½ t oat bran (7.5 ml)

5 T fat-free or low-fat milk (75 ml)

3 T fat-free or low-fat plain
    yoghurt (50 g)

ice cubes (optional, but unnecessary
    if frozen berries are used)

Place all the ingredients in a blender
and blend until smooth.

Food fact Berries not only give this
    smoothie the highest fibre con-
    tent, but they also provide gener-
    ous amounts of phyto-nutrients
    and antioxidants.

GO-GO JUICE

1 small apple (75 g)

1 small banana (80 g)

1 small pear (110 g)

5 T low-fat milk (75 ml)

5 T fat-free vanilla yoghurt (75 ml)

2 t Nesquik cream soda powder (7 g)

ice cubes (optional)

Place all the ingredients in a blender
and blend until smooth.

Food fact Milk flavouring powders
(chocolate, strawberry, cream
soda, and so on) should be added
to smoothies in small amounts.
They are a concentrated source
of sugar and should only be used
to add a hint of flavour.

MANGO MANIA

1 small or ½ large fresh mango
    (150 g) or

10 strips dried mango, rehydrated
    in water

100 g pineapple (1 x 2½ cm slice)

100 ml plain low-fat yoghurt

3 T fat-free/skimmed milk (50 ml)

1 t sesame seeds (5 ml)

1 t linseeds (5 ml)

ice cubes (optional)

Place all the ingredients in a blender
and blend until smooth.

Food fact On average, seeds
    contain 30% fat and nuts contain
    50% fat.

Berry-licious smoothie.

MEALS-IN-A-GLASS

These are not ideal as meal replacements because they are formulated from highly processed ingredients. However, rather than skipping a meal, use a well-balanced meal replacement mix. The best way to assess the quality of such a drink, is to assess the nutritional information given on the product.

It is important to check the nutritional values per serving, and not per 100 g. For example, adding 50 g powder to a glass of water should result in a meal-in-a-glass that meets as near as possible the criteria given above for a balanced smoothie.

If you are not adding water to the powder, but rather fruit juice or milk, the following values need to be added to those of the single serving of powder:

☐ 250 ml fruit juice = 500 kJ plus 33 g carbohydrate

☐ 250 ml low-fat milk = 520 kJ plus 12 g carbohydrate plus 8 g protein plus 5 g fat

☐ 250 ml skimmed milk = 365 kJ plus 12 g carbohydrate plus 8 g protein plus 0.5 g fat

☐ 250 ml low-fat soya milk = 470 kJ plus 15 g carbohydrate plus 8 g protein plus 3 g fat

Meals-in-a-glass should not be too high in protein as the body needs adequate carbohydrate to utilise the protein effectively. In order to control this, each gram of protein should be matched with at least two grams of carbohydrate. Check that the ratio of protein to carbohydrate is at least 1:2. This means that high protein shakes should usually be mixed with diluted fruit juice, or a fruit should be eaten with the high-protein shake prepared with water.

See the Appendix on page 183 for the checklist for smoothies and meals-in-a-glass.

three
LUNCHES
& DINNERS

Lunches and dinners, whether eaten at home or packed to take to work, should meet the requirements of a balanced meal on a plate. Always consider the balanced meal on a plate and keep to these proportions, no matter where you are eating.

Quick roast chicken dinner. (Recipe on page 65.)

BALANCED LUNCHES AND DINNERS

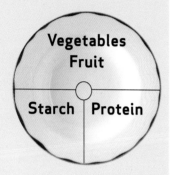

Step 1 Half-fill your plate with colour from nature's colour palette in the form of fruit or vegetables such as roasted vegetables, cooked vegetables or salad vegetables.

Step 2 Choose one fistful of starch in the form of low-GI cooked starches (rice, baby potatoes, sweet potatoes, mealies, corn, and so on) in the case of dinner, and perhaps low-GI breads or rolls, or cold cooked starches for packed lunches.

Step 3 Choose one portion (the size of the palm of your hand) of low-fat dairy or lean protein such as low-fat cheese, boiled egg, tuna or chicken breast.

Step 4 Have a small portion of healthy fat such as one teaspoon of olive oil in salad dressings, a small handful of nuts or seeds, two tablespoons of peanut butter, or a quarter of an avocado. Alternatively, a small amount of good quality oil could be used to prepare the protein of the meal.

In this section we will show you how easy it is to assemble nutritious, balanced meals using easy-to-prepare foods.

GUIDELINES FOR ASSEMBLING BALANCED, HEALTHY MEALS

☐ Dry groceries can be bought on a monthly basis but fresh foods need to be purchased twice a week. Plan two short shopping trips every week, even if you pop into the shops on your way home from work. Ordering online is another convenient option.

☐ Pre-prepared vegetables are useful but should be used within two days in order to retain the nutritional value.

☐ Home-made vegetable soups are a smart way to add generous amounts of vegetables to a meal. Make vegetable soups in bulk and freeze in smaller batches.

☐ Roasting vegetables in larger quantities and keeping them chilled for a few days makes for quick reheating and adding to meals, or for instant use in salads.

☐ Fruit can be kept in the fridge for up to a week.

☐ Cooked starches such as rice, pasta, *stampkoring* (crushed or pearled wheat), barley and mealies can be cooked in larger quantities and stored in the fridge for up to a week and frozen for up to a month.

☐ Chicken fillets and hard-boiled eggs can also be prepared in larger quantities and stored in the fridge for up to a week.

☐ When cooking savoury mince, make more than is needed. Freeze in smaller portions, about half a cup (125 ml). Ready-cooked mince can be added to cooked sweet potato or tinned chickpeas, or piled on top of seed loaf toast or into a mini pita pocket with lots of salad vegetables.

☐ Meal leftovers can be stored in microwave-safe containers for quick and easy balanced meals on the run.

☐ Ready-made sauces such as curry, korma, mushroom, tomato-basil, lemon and herb, sweet and sour, olive and sun-dried tomato, relish, and so on should have a fat content of 3 g or less per 100 g to ensure that you do not add appreciable amounts of fat to the meal. In addition, use only half the amount of sauce per serving. This means that you would use twice the amount of meat, fish, chicken or vegetables recommended on the product so that you end up using half the amount of sauce advised. Any leftovers can be chilled or frozen for another meal.

☐ Ready-made higher fat ingredients such as low-oil mayonnaise, curry pastes, atchar, pesto, olive tapenade and hummus should be added with discretion and in very small amounts to avoid adding too much fat to your meal.

☐ Sweet-chilli sauce, chutney, relishes, fruit preserves such as green fig preserve, onion marmalade, and so on may be fat free but have a very high sugar content. Use no more than two tablespoons per person, to keep within the sugar recommendation of no more than 10 g sugar per meal.

☐ Keep a variety of plastic containers, resealable plastic bags, small cooler boxes, ice bricks, water bottles, mini sauce containers with tight-fitting lids and wipes on hand.

☐ If you have access to a fridge at work, start each week by taking along a container with assembled lunch basics. Include salad vegetables such as cherry tomatoes, small cucumbers, sweet peppers and other crudités. Add cottage cheese, cheese wedges, hard-boiled eggs, tuna in brine, small tins of baked beans, high-fibre crackers, yoghurts, etc. (See the shopping list at the end of this section, page 68.) Assembling your own lunch from your supply of basics will be faster than fighting the canteen queues or walking across the road to a local takeaway. Your assembled lunch will also be healthier and sustain your energy throughout the afternoon.

GUIDELINES FOR READY-MADE MEALS

☐ Ready-made single meal portions are often too big. Choose those that are no larger than 250 g per serving.

☐ Ready-made meals usually provide only the starch and meat (protein) of the meal. To balance the ready-made meal, at least as much salad or vegetables should be added.

☐ Salad bars and deli counter salads are usually high in fat due to the dressings used. Make sure you choose salads without mayonnaise or oily dressings. For example, beetroot salad, mixed lettuce-type salads, carrot salad, or pickled vegetables (gherkins, Peppadews, cabbage, mushrooms, and so on). The amount of undressed salads on your plate should be at least as much as the ready-made meal serving.

☐ When choosing ready-cooked vegetables at a deli counter, choose a variety of colours and ensure that these make up at least half of your meal.

☐ Avoid those vegetables prepared with oil and cream, such as creamed spinach, oily roast vegetables, fried brinjals and other fried vegetables.

☐ Roast potatoes, sweet potatoes, pumpkin fritters and dumplings are starches and not vegetables.

☐ When choosing sandwiches, hamburgers and wraps choose those with lots of lettuce, tomato, cucumber, grated carrot and other salad vegetables in order to get as much colour as possible.

☐ For meals-in-a-glass, refer to the information at the end of the Breakfasts section on page 44.

☐ If a nutritional analysis is provided:
  • Check the energy (kJ) and fat content per serving. Be careful to look at the "per serving" values and not the "per 100 g".

  • Energy should be between 1 500 kJ and 1 800 kJ per serving for women, and between 1 800 kJ and 2 200 kJ for men. The fat should be no more than 15 g per serving for both men and women.

  • If the energy and fat are within these recommendations, the carbohydrate and protein will more than likely be within suitable limits; protein about 25 g and carbohydrate about 40 g per serving.

  • For added benefit the fibre content should be about 5 g or more, per serving.

☐ For a checklist of the criteria for buying a meal on the run, see the Appendix on page 183.

All the meal suggestions below are amounts for one adult woman. Men would eat 1½ times these amounts. This means the vegetables also need to be increased, not only the starch and protein!

SMOKED SALMON LIGHT MEAL
(pictured)

Energy 1 238 kJ; carbohydrate 30 g; fibre 8 g; protein 15 g; fat 12 g
Equivalent to 1 starch; 2 proteins; 1 fruit; 1 vegetable

1 Thread 2 thin slices of smoked salmon (40 g) onto a kebab skewer, alternating with a peeled and quartered kiwi fruit.
2 Spread 1 T flavoured cream cheese onto a slice of low-GI seed loaf.
3 Serve with generous amounts of rocket and mixed lettuce leaves, a few halved baby tomatoes and some cucumber.
4 Sprinkle with fresh lemon juice to serve.

Assembling tip Smoked trout fillets or smoked beef can be used instead of the smoked salmon.

Food fact Although flavoured cream cheese is high in fat, using only one tablespoon on a slice of bread instead of margarine or butter, not only adds depth of flavour, but also does not push the fat content of the meal up too much.

BEETROOT, PEAR AND BILTONG SALAD

Energy 1 631 kJ; carbohydrate 43 g; fibre 11 g; protein 22 g; fat 13 g
Equivalent to 3 proteins; 2 fruits (starch); 3 vegetables

1 Toss together 5 quartered precooked baby beetroot (150g), a handful of cherry tomatoes, a handful of baby mushrooms and 1 peeled and cubed pear.
2 Top with 2 T shredded lean biltong.
3 Crumble ¼ of a round of feta cheese on top.
4 Drizzle with 1 T prepared blue cheese salad dressing.

Smoked salmon light meal.

Assembling tip Bottled baby
   beetroot is a reasonable
   substitute for fresh precooked
   beetroot.

Food facts For a vegetarian meal,
   leave out the biltong and use half
   a round of feta cheese.
   Lean biltong provides a good
   source of protein for meals.
   Ostrich and venison biltong are
   the leaner choices, although lean
   beef biltong is also acceptable.
   The fibre content of meals can
   easily be increased by adding a
   piece of fresh fruit to the meal,
   incorporated into the meal or
   added as a "dessert".

TANGY CHICKPEA SALAD
Energy 1 376 kJ; carbohydrate 42 g;
fibre 11 g; protein 11 g; fat 12 g
Equivalent to 2 starches; 1 protein;
½ fruit; ½ vegetable; 2 fats

1   Place 2 generous handfuls of
    mixed salad leaves and fresh
    herbs into a salad bowl.
2   Add ½ red pepper, sliced into
    strips, and a few red onion rings.
3   Add ½ tin drained chickpeas.
    If you do not like chickpeas,
    serve with 1 slice of seed loaf.
4   Toss in 1 handful of fresh berries
    of your choice.
5   Top with 4 anchovies.
6   Sprinkle with 2 T honey and
    mustard dressing.

Assembling tip Store leftover chickpeas in a sealed container (not in the opened tin) in the fridge for up to a week or make into hummus for another assembled meal (see page 59).

Food facts To make a meal of a salad, ensure that there is at least one starch and some protein in the salad. However, salads served as starters should not contain the starch and protein, as these are both provided by the main meal. In this salad, most of the protein is provided by the chickpeas and not the anchovies. The strong flavour of the anchovies limits the amount that can be used. Most of the fat in this salad comes from the dressing as most ready-made salad dressings contain 30% fat.

ROAST VEGETABLE AND COUSCOUS SALAD

Energy 1 353 kJ; carbohydrate 32 g; fibre 16 g; protein 14 g; fat 16 g
Equivalent to 1 starch; 1½ proteins/dairy; 2 vegetables; 2 fats

1 Place 3 T couscous in a heatproof bowl that you can use for serving the salad. Add a shake of herb salt. Pour over 4 T boiling water and leave for about 5 minutes to hydrate. Fluff up the couscous using a fork.
2 Add 1½ cups roasted vegetables (either prepared at home or bought from a deli counter). Suitable vegetables for roasting include butternut, courgettes, patty pans, cherry tomatoes, peppers, mushrooms, onion, cauliflower, broccoli, carrots and leeks.
3 Stir in chopped mint and coriander leaves.
4 Top with ½ round of herbed feta cheese, crumbled or cubed.

Assembling tips This salad can be served warm in winter to provide a hot meal.
To save time and energy fill your largest baking tray with the vegetables to be roasted. When cool, freeze the leftovers (for up to a month), or refrigerate (for up to one week) in 1½ cup (375 ml) labelled containers. See page 65 for how to roast vegetables.

Food facts Couscous is one of the most concentrated starches. The 3 T uncooked couscous in this salad provide a whole starch portion.
The fibre in the vegetables gives this meal its exceptionally high fibre content.

WALDORF SALAD

Energy 1 490 kJ; carbohydrate 43 g;
fibre 8 g; protein 10 g; fat 15 g
Equivalent to 2 fruits (starch);
1 dairy/protein; 2½ fats

1 Cube 3 thick slices of cucumber
   and mix with 1 chopped green
   apple and 1 T fruit juice of your
   choice.
2 Add 1 small chopped pear and
   1 stick of chopped celery.
3 Cube 1 matchbox of fat-reduced
   cheese and sprinkle over the
   salad.
4 Top with 3 pecan or walnut
   halves.
5 Mix 1 T low-oil mayonnaise with
   1 T balsamic vinegar and use this
   as the dressing for the salad.

Food facts The fruit in this salad
provides the "starch" for this
meal.
Regular Waldorf salad is a high-
fat meal because of the cheese,
nuts and salad dressing. With
this salad it is important to
adhere to the amounts given for
these ingredients, in order to
keep the fat content within the
recommendations.

ITALIAN PESTO TOAST WITH SALAD (pictured)

Energy 1 410 kJ; carbohydrate 35 g;
fibre 7 g; protein 24 g; fat 13 g
Equivalent to 1 starch; 1 low-fat dairy;
2 proteins; 2 vegetables

1 Toast 1 slice rye bread and
   spread with 2 t ready-made
   pesto.
2 Layer with 1 thinly sliced tomato,
   overlapping the slices to fill the
   slice of bread.
3 Scrunch a generous amount
   (65 g) of shaved lean turkey or
   chicken on top of the leaves.
4 Top with 1 matchbox of grated
   mozzarella cheese. Season to
   taste and place under a hot grill
   until the cheese just melts.
5 Serve with a large tossed salad
   splashed with balsamic vinegar.

Food fact Shaved cold meats are
all very lean and because they
are sliced so thinly, generous
amounts (half a 125 g packet
per person) can be used as the
protein in meals.

Italian pesto toast with salad.

CRUDITÉS ON THE RUN (pictured)
Energy 1 624 kJ; carbohydrate 42 g;
fibre 16 g; protein 19 g; fat 15 g
Equivalent to 1 starch; 2 lean proteins;
3 vegetables; 2 fats

1 Fill a dinner plate or lunchbox
with a variety of easy-to-eat
finger veggies such as cherry
tomatoes, snap peas or mange
touts, baby carrots, baby corn,
mushrooms, broccoli florets,
cauliflower florets and gherkins
(2-3 handfuls or cups).
2 Add 6 T lower fat hummus and
½ cup tzatziki (grated cucumber
and plain yoghurt) and use as a
dip for the vegetables.
3 For men, add 3–4 Provitas.

Assembling tip Although
hummus, including lower fat
hummus, is readily available in
supermarkets, it is quick and
easy to make at home.

Hummus recipe Drain 1 tin of
chickpeas and pour into a
liquidiser or food processor.
Add 4 T lemon juice, 1 t (or more)
crushed garlic, 4 T tahini or
peanut butter and seasoning of
your choice. Blend until smooth
and serve. Hummus can be stored
in a sealed container in the fridge
for up to a week.

Food fact Most of the fat in this
meal comes from the controlled
portion of the lower fat hummus.
Regular hummus contains at
least double the fat of the lower
fat version because of the added
oil, so be sure to always choose
the lower fat hummus or make
your own, without any added oil.

TRICOLOR SWEETCORN SALAD
Energy 1 161 kJ; carbohydrate 29 g;
fibre 10 g; protein 13 g; fat 12 g
Equivalent to 1½ starches; 1 protein;
1½ vegetables; 1½ fats

1 Chop 2 cups of the following
together: spring onion, cucumber,
tomato, red and yellow peppers.
2 Add ½ tin whole-kernel
sweetcorn, drained.
3 Add 3 sliced calamata olives.
4 Chop up 1 hard-boiled egg and
add to the salad.
5 Mix 1 T low-oil mayonnaise with
1 t lemon juice to make a
dressing. Add a little water if the
dressing is too thick.

Assembling tip Boiled eggs keep
for at least a week in the fridge
and are easy to add as a protein
to any meal. To save energy, boil
six eggs at a time.

Crudités on the run.

SWEET POTATO SPUD

Energy 1 657 kJ; carbohydrate 57 g; fibre 9 g; protein 18 g; fat 10 g
Equivalent to 2½ starches; 1½ low-fat dairy; 1 vegetable; 1 fat

1 Place 1 medium sweet potato in the microwave and cook for a few minutes until soft.
2 While the sweet potato is cooking, mix ½ cup of chunky cottage cheese with ½ cup of finely chopped salad vegetables such as peppers, celery, tomato, cucumber, and grated carrot.
3 Add 1 t Dijon or wholegrain mustard.
4 Cut open the sweet potato and fill with the chunky cottage cheese mixture.
5 Serve with a small tossed salad dressed with 1 T low-oil mayonnaise thinned out with lemon juice or vinegar.

Assembling tip Mix the whole tub of cottage cheese with double the amount of finely chopped vegetables. Use half for this meal and keep the other half for another quick light meal. Pile the prepared cottage cheese mixture on a slice of low-GI bread and serve with a salad.

WARM MIXED VEGETABLE AND TUNA SALAD

Energy 1 467 kJ; carbohydrate 40 g; fibre 10 g; protein 29 g; fat 7 g
Equivalent to 2 starches; 3½ lean proteins; 1 vegetable; 1 fat

1 Place 1 cup of mixed frozen or tinned vegetables (corn, peas and carrots) in a microwavable bowl.
2 Drain 1 tin of tuna in brine (175 g) and add half to the vegetables.
3 Microwave on high for 3 minutes until warmed through.
4 Stir in 2 T low-oil mayonnaise and 2 T sweet-chilli sauce.
5 Season to taste with salt, pepper and herbs of your choice.

Assembling tip Store the leftover tuna in a sealed container in the fridge for up to three days and then use to make this quick and easy meal again.

Food fact Tuna and chicken are more concentrated sources of lean protein than red meat or eggs. For this reason, a small portion of chicken or fish is enough to provide the protein for a balanced meal.

MEXICAN TORTILLA MEAL

Energy 1 727 kJ; carbohydrate 39 g;
fibre 7 g; protein 22 g; fat 18 g
Equivalent to 1½ starches; 2½ proteins;
3 vegetables; 1 fat

1 Sprinkle 1 tortilla with a little
   water and warm in a tea towel in
   the microwave for 20 seconds
   on high. Alternatively, warm the
   dampened tortilla in a frying pan.
2 Heat 1 c ready-made salsa.
3 While the salsa is heating, place
   the warm tortilla on a plate and
   spread mixed lettuce leaves,
   coriander leaves and thin
   cucumber slices on top.
4 Place a chunkily chopped hard-
   boiled egg and ¼ sliced avocado
   pear in the middle.
5 Thin out 4 T fat-free smooth
   cottage cheese with a little
   water or skimmed milk and
   drizzle over the filling.
6 Top with the warm salsa and roll
   up the tortilla.

Food fact Regular tortilla meals
   are high in fat because of the
   sour cream, Cheddar cheese and
   guacamole (avocado). In this
   version, all of these have been
   controlled or changed. Despite
   this, the fat content is still
   slightly over the recommended
   fat content for a healthy meal.

POLENTA AND TOMATO GRILL

Energy 1 473 kJ; carbohydrate 51 g;
fibre 1.7 g; protein 13 g; fat 11 g
Equivalent to 1 starch; 1 dairy;
5 vegetables; 1 fat

1 Cube 1 thin slice of ready-cooked
   polenta (finger thickness or 55 g)
   and place on a dinner plate.
2 Spoon over 1 cup of ready-made
   herbed tomato sauce (bottled or
   tinned).
3 Top with 1 matchbox grated
   mozzarella and 1 t grated
   Parmesan cheese.
4 Place under the grill until hot and
   bubbling.
5 Serve with a salad to fill your
   dinner plate generously and
   drizzle with oil-free dressing.

Food fact Parmesan cheese may
   be higher in fat but the strong
   flavour allows you to use just
   a little for maximum flavour
   enhancement. Grated Parmesan
   keeps for months in the
   refrigerator.

HALLOUMI CHEESE ON TOAST
(Pictured on page 4)
Energy 1 771 kJ; carbohydrate 44 g;
fibre 8.5 g; protein 22 g; fat 15 g
Equivalent to 2 starches; 2 dairy/
proteins; 2 vegetables

1 Microwave ½ c broccoli florets
   for 3 minutes on high. Set aside.
2 Toast 1 slice of seed loaf.
3 Heat 1 T soya sauce with 2 T
   sweet-chilli sauce in a frying pan
   until bubbly.
4 Add 3 finger slices of halloumi
   cheese (2 matchboxes) and fry
   gently for 1 minute on each side.
5 Place the "fried" halloumi slices
   on the toast.
6 Serve with ½ c ready-made
   beetroot salad and the broccoli
   florets.

Assembling tip As an alternative to
   the beetroot salad and broccoli,
   add a large tossed salad.

Food fact Soya sauce and halloumi
   cheese are both high in sodium,
   which means that those who have
   high blood pressure should use
   as little soya sauce as possible.

PESTO TOMATOES
(pictured)
Energy 1 592 kJ; carbohydrate 40 g;
fibre 6 g; protein 14 g; fat 14 g
Equivalent to 2 starches; 1½ dairy/
proteins; 1½ vegetables; 1½ fats

1 Cut 2 large tomatoes in half and
   slice away the rounded sides so
   that the 4 halves can rest level on
   a plate.
2 Top each tomato half with
   1 t ready-made pesto and ½ t
   tapenade or 2 chopped olives for
   all 4 tomato halves.
3 Place a thin slice of mozzarella or
   brie cheese on top of the pesto
   and olives (use only 1 matchbox
   of cheese for all 4 tomato
   halves).
4 Grill the tomatoes until the
   cheese bubbles.
5 Serve on a bed of baby spinach
   mixed with rocket leaves and 3 mini
   pita pockets (heated under the
   grill). Season with black pepper.

Food fact This (lacto) vegetarian
   meal contains enough
   protein, thanks to the cheese.
   Traditionally, vegetarian meals
   are thought to be lacking in
   protein. However, it is vitamin
   B12 and iron that are lacking
   more often than protein.

Pesto tomatoes.

ROAST VEGETABLE AND FETA PITA

(pictured)

Energy 1 761 kJ; carbohydrate 49 g;
fibre 11 g; protein 14 g; fat 14 g
Equivalent to 3 starches; 1 dairy/
protein; 1½ vegetables; 1 fat.

1 Place 250 g (2 c) ready-to-
   roast, roasting vegetables in an
   ovenproof dish with a lid.
2 Add 1 t olive oil, a sprig of
   rosemary or fresh thyme (or
   ½ t dried rosemary/thyme) and
   ½ t salt. With the lid firmly on the
   dish, shake the vegetables until
   they are well coated.
3 Microwave for 10 minutes and
   then grill without the lid under a
   hot grill for 10 minutes, tossing
   the vegetables after 5 minutes.
4 When done, roughly crumble
   30 g feta cheese (1 matchbox)
   over the hot vegetables and stir
   through.
5 Drizzle with ready-made low-
   oil Greek dressing (10 ml or 2 t),
   and serve hot or cold with 1 pita
   pocket half or 3 mini pita pockets.

QUICK ROAST CHICKEN DINNER

(pictured on page 46)

Energy 1 630 kJ; carbohydrate 26 g;
fibre 11 g; protein 42 g; fat 12 g
Equivalent to 1½ starches; 5 low-fat
proteins; 1½ vegetables

1 Cook 3 baby potatoes or 2 mini
   corn on the cob in the microwave
   (pricked and microwaved for
   2 minutes on high, covered).
2 Microwave or cook 2 c frozen or
   fresh vegetable medley (broccoli,
   butternut, sweet peppers, onion,
   courgettes, patty pans, etc.).
3 Place the cooked vegetables and
   potatoes on a dinner plate. Add
   prepared roast chicken pieces
   that are the size of the palm of
   your hand. Remove the skin.
4 Pour 2 T low-fat ready-
   made cheese sauce over the
   vegetables.
5 Cover and reheat the chicken
   dinner in the microwave for
   30-60 seconds.

Food fact Chicken is a very
concentrated source of lean
protein. A portion the size of
the palm of your hand therefore
contains more than enough protein
for any meal.

Roast vegetable and feta pita with fruit-infused water.

SPICY GRILLED CHICKEN WITH ROAST VEG AND SWEET POTATO

Energy 1 660 kJ; carbohydrate 26 g;
fibre 8 g; protein 39 g; fat 15 g
Equivalent to 1½ starches; 4½ low-fat
proteins; 1 vegetable; 1 fat

1   Cook $\frac{1}{3}$ c ready-peeled and
    cubed sweet potato or 3 baby
    potatoes until soft.
2   Lightly cook 1 c fresh or frozen
    prepared vegetables until just
    tender. Your vegetable mix
    should include a lot of colour:
    broccoli, carrots, courgettes,
    onion, butternut, cauliflower,
    green, yellow and red peppers,
    mushrooms, leeks.
3   Generously sprinkle your
    favourite spice over 4 chicken
    breasts (thaw first if frozen).
4   Place the chicken in a large oven-
    proof dish and add the cooked
    sweet potato and vegetables.
    Drizzle with 1 t olive oil.
5   Cover and bake or microwave
    until the chicken is cooked.
6   Serve only 1 chicken breast
    drizzled with 2 T ready-made
    cheese sauce, all the potato and
    the veggies. Use the rest of the
    chicken in other meals.

STIR-FRY

Energy 1 842 kJ; carbohydrate 46 g;
fibre 11 g; protein 31 g; fat 14 g
Equivalent to 2½ starches; 3½ proteins;
2 vegetables; 1 fat

1   Heat 1 t olive oil in a large frying
    pan or wok.
2   Add ¼ chopped onion and 1 t
    crushed garlic and 1 t crushed
    ginger. Gently stir-fry and then
    add 3 matchboxes lean steak
    strips.
3   Stir-fry until just cooked and
    then add 3 c fresh or frozen
    prepared stir-fry vegetables
    (bean sprouts, broccoli florets,
    shredded cabbage, mushrooms,
    mange touts/snap peas, sliced
    peppers, chopped spinach, sliced
    courgettes).
4   Add ½ c frozen or tinned
    sweetcorn, and mix.
5   While the stir-fry is cooking,
    combine the following in a cup:
    1 t brown sugar, 1 t soya sauce,
    2 t lemon juice and enough water
    to fill the cup. Pour over the stir-
    fry and heat through.
6   Serve without adding any other
    starch.

Food facts Restaurant stir-fries are usually high in fat because of the amount of oil used. When making stir-fries at home, use only 1 t oil to stir-fry the vegetables.
The sauce of a stir-fry adds starch because of the sugar it contains.

PIZZA MEAL

Energy 1 563 kJ; carbohydrate 41 g; fibre 7.5 g; protein 19 g; fat 15 g
Equivalent to 2 starches; 2 dairy/proteins; 1½ vegetables; 2 fats

1 Reheat 2 slices of leftover pizza.
2 Serve with a generous tossed salad drizzled with 1 T low-oil dressing or balsamic vinegar.

Assembling tips Pizzas are high in fat, so choose one with several vegetable toppings (mushrooms, peppers, asparagus, onion, spinach, etc.) and only one protein topping (sausage, bacon, salami, ham, seafood, etc.).
The best way to reheat pizza is under a (table-top) grill. Microwaving tends to make the pizza tough.

FISH AND CHIPS

Energy 1 709 kJ; carbohydrate 37 g; fibre 7 g; protein 37 g; fat 13 g
Equivalent to 2 starches; 4 low-fat proteins; 1 vegetable; 2 fats

1 Place one fistful (10 chips or 100 g) oven-ready frozen chips on a baking tray. There is no need to add any oil. Bake according to the instructions on the packet.
2 Ten minutes before the chips are done, place 2 frozen flavoured or spiced (not crumbed) fish pieces on the same baking tray as the chips and bake until done.
3 Serve with a large tossed green salad drizzled with 2 T low-oil salad dressing and tomato sauce (optional) for the chips.

Food facts Chips are a high-fat food. Even oven chips baked without any extra oil, contain approximately 2 t fat per 100 g, which is only 10 chips! Restaurant and takeaway chips are not only high in fat, but also contain harmful trans fats. For this reason it is better to enjoy a small portion of oven chips prepared at home.

SHOPPING LIST FOR LUNCHES AND DINNERS

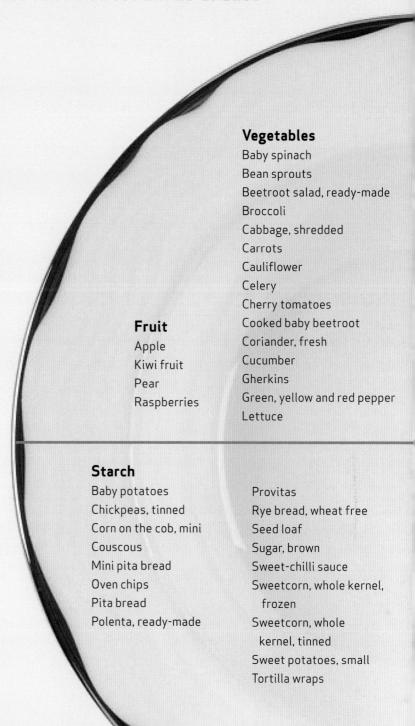

Fats
Avocado
Blue cheese dressing
Cheese sauce, fat reduced,
  ready-made
Honey mustard dressing
Hummus, low fat
Light salad dressings
Low-oil mayonnaise
Olive oil
Olives
Pecan nuts or walnuts
Pesto, ready-made

Fruit
Apple
Kiwi fruit
Pear
Raspberries

Vegetables
Baby spinach
Bean sprouts
Beetroot salad, ready-made
Broccoli
Cabbage, shredded
Carrots
Cauliflower
Celery
Cherry tomatoes
Cooked baby beetroot
Coriander, fresh
Cucumber
Gherkins
Green, yellow and red pepper
Lettuce

Starch
Baby potatoes
Chickpeas, tinned
Corn on the cob, mini
Couscous
Mini pita bread
Oven chips
Pita bread
Polenta, ready-made

Provitas
Rye bread, wheat free
Seed loaf
Sugar, brown
Sweet-chilli sauce
Sweetcorn, whole kernel,
  frozen
Sweetcorn, whole
  kernel, tinned
Sweet potatoes, small
Tortilla wraps

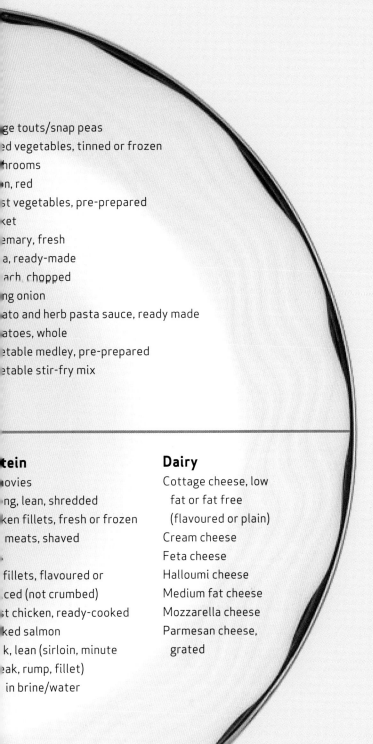

ge touts/snap peas
ed vegetables, tinned or frozen
hrooms
n, red
st vegetables, pre-prepared
ket
emary, fresh
a, ready-made
ach, chopped
ng onion
ato and herb pasta sauce, ready made
atoes, whole
etable medley, pre-prepared
etable stir-fry mix

Condiments

Balsamic vinegar
Garlic, crushed
Ginger, crushed
Herb salt
Herbs, fresh
Lemon juice
Mustard
Soya sauce
Tomato sauce
Tzatziki

tein
ovies
ng, lean, shredded
ken fillets, fresh or frozen
meats, shaved

fillets, flavoured or
ced (not crumbed)
st chicken, ready-cooked
ked salmon
k, lean (sirloin, minute
eak, rump, fillet)
in brine/water

Dairy

Cottage cheese, low
   fat or fat free
   (flavoured or plain)
Cream cheese
Feta cheese
Halloumi cheese
Medium fat cheese
Mozzarella cheese
Parmesan cheese,
   grated

four
SMART SNACKING

I n today's fast-paced world where there is often no time to prepare snacks and meals, it is important to learn how to snack smartly using readily available food items and to combine them correctly. Smart snacking stabilises blood sugar levels, which promotes effective cognitive function and good health. Stable blood sugar levels help to manage inappropriate food cravings, maintain metabolic rate, and therefore promote weight management.

Cheese and fruit or vegetable skewers on page 77.

WHAT IS A SMART SNACK?

☐ A smart snack should fit into your hand. After all, it is a snack and not a meal.

☐ Each snack should contain about 500 kJ for women and 750 kJ for men.

☐ The carbohydrate content should be no more than 25 g for women and 35 g for men.

☐ The fat content should be about 10 g per snack (although for weight loss closer to 5 g is better).

☐ The fibre content should preferably be at least 2 g fibre per snack.

☐ A smart snack should be slow release (low GI < 62) as well as low GL (GL 7-10)*.

For an overview of the GI and the GL see page 74.

READING THE LABEL

Step 1 Check the weight of the snack portion you will be eating.

Step 2 Turn the snack over to find the nutritional analysis.

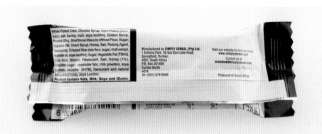

Step 3 Look for the list of ingredients, usually in small print.

Step 1 Determine the weight of the snack you will be eating. Remember to check that the actual weight of the snack is the same as the weight per serving given in the nutritional table. If it is not the same, you will have to calculate the nutritional values of your snack from the per 100 g column.

Step 2 Look at the nutritional analysis table and compare the nutrients per snack with the criteria for a smart snack. Ideally all the criteria should be met. The fibre content may not always be attainable.

SMART SNACK CRITERIA	SAMPLE SNACK	COMMENTS
500 kJ (women); 750 kJ (men)	740 kJ	Too high for women
10 g fat (5 g fat for weight management)	7.2 g	Acceptable
25 g carbohydrate (women); 35 g (men)	22.5 g	Acceptable
Preferably 2 g fibre per snack	2 g	Acceptable

Conclusion Many health bars weigh 40 g or even more, which is too big a portion for women. The ideal serving size for this example would be a 30 g bar. This bar is not ideal for a woman but would be all right for a man. See page 112 in the Portion Distortion section for a discussion on snack portion sizes.

Step 3 This last step will enable you to determine the impact the snack will have on your blood sugar levels. In order to get an idea whether the snack bar is slow release (low GI) or not, you need to check the list of ingredients. Since all ingredients on foods in South Africa are listed in order of mass with the heaviest one listed first and the lightest one listed last, the first third of the ingredients on the list will give an indication of what the GI of the snack will be.

In the sample snack the first third of the ingredients are: oats, syrup, sugar, water.

Oats – low GI (53)
Syrup – intermediate GI (63)
Sugar – intermediate GI (65)
Water – no GI effect

Therefore the net effect on blood sugar levels would be a slower release of glucose from the snack (intermediate GI of approximately 62).

To look up the GI values of most commonly eaten foods in South Africa, use *The South African Glycemic Index and Load Guide* by G Steenkamp and L Delport (GIFSA, 2010). It is available from most bookstores, some pharmacies and dieticians and from the websites www.gabisteenkamp.co.za and www.gifoundation.com.

THE LOWDOWN ON THE GLYCEMIC INDEX (GI) AND THE GLYCEMIC LOAD (GL)

The GI gives an indication of how fast a food that contains carbohydrate, affects our blood sugar levels. All carbohydrates are not equal. There are those that are digested and absorbed slowly over about three hours and those that spike blood sugar levels almost immediately. Low-GI foods take three hours to be digested and absorbed and therefore supply the body with a steady source of fuel (glucose) for up to three hours.

High-GI foods, on the other hand, will invariably spike blood sugar levels, resulting in higher insulin levels that encourage fat storage and irritability and reduce cognitive function as the body tries to rectify the high blood sugar levels. Slow-release foods include vegetables, most fruit, seed breads, legumes such as baked beans and hummus, and many other unprocessed foods.

The GL by contrast, gives an indication of the glucose load the body has to deal with in order to keep blood sugar levels within normal limits. Snacks are meant to keep body fuel levels in a steady state, rather than push blood sugar levels up. The bigger the portion, the larger the glycemic load, and the harder it is for the body to correct the glucose surge. A glycemic load of less than 10 is easily metabolised by the body and that is why snacks should have a load of around 10.

GL = Carbohydrate per serving x GI/100.

In the above example, the 40 g bar would have a load of 14 (22.5 x 62/100 = 13.9).

A 30 g portion of the same bar would have a GL of 10 (16.8 x 62/100 = 10.4).

GUIDELINES FOR SMART SNACKING

☐ Plan ahead – use the smart snack criteria to choose smart snacks. Keep a laminated copy of these smart snack criteria with you when shopping.

☐ Shop ahead – on most days you would need a morning and an afternoon snack. While doing your normal grocery shopping buy a variety of perhaps 10 or 20 non-perishable snacks such as dried fruit, nuts, mini health bars, low-GI rusks (see the biscotti recipe in the Appendix on page 187), (low-GI) crackers, and so on.

☐ As fresh fruit is perfectly packaged, nutritious and the ideal snack, buy a bag of apples at the start of the week and leave it in the office fridge. Make sure you finish the apples by the end of the week. The next week try naartjies, then pears, peaches, and so on.

☐ When fresh fruit is not available, stew a whole packet of dried fruit and store in the refrigerator. Use half a cup of stewed fruit as a snack.

☐ Your fresh snacks can then be interspersed with the non-perishable snacks.

☐ Make sure your smart snacks are close at hand: in your desk drawer, the cubbyhole of the car, your briefcase, gym bag, or handbag.

☐ Many fresh snacks such as boiled eggs, chicken fillets, fruit salad, home-made low-GI muffins, biscuits and rusks can be made in larger quantities and used throughout the week.

☐ If needed, a meal can be replaced with two or three snacks for a woman and three or four snacks for a man.

SMART SNACKING IDEAS

All the ideas listed below meet the criteria for smart snacks for women. Men could have 1½ times these amounts.

☐ **Biltong** – about 30 g leaner biltong such as ostrich or game.

☐ **Biscuits** – two biscuits, home-made low GI and low fat (see recipe in the Appendix on page 186).

☐ **Boiled egg with three or four crackers**.

☐ **Cereal** – mini packet of high-fibre cereal such as muesli, about 30 g.

☐ **Cheese and crackers** – buy the individual packs of three or four crackers and use two wedges of processed cheese.

☐ **Cheese and fruit** – one matchbox of low-fat cheese with one fresh fruit or two pieces of dried fruit, for example brie and kiwi slices.

☐ **Cheese and fruit skewers** – for example, two black grapes per mini mozzarella ball threaded alternately onto a skewer.

☐ **Cheese and vegetable skewers** – for example, two cherry tomatoes per mini cheese cube threaded alternately onto a skewer.

☐ **Cold meat and fruit** – one strip of Parma ham wrapped around a melon wedge, or four shaved turkey slices with four prunes or dried apricots.

☐ **Cottage cheese** – three tablespoons with five dried mango strips or fresh kiwi slices.

☐ **Crudités and dip** – one to two cups of vegetable crudités with up to six tablespoons of fat-free flavoured cottage cheese, tzatziki or reduced fat hummus. To make your own low-fat hummus, see page 59.

☐ **Dried fruit** – serving of about 40 g.

☐ **Drinking yoghurts** – fat-free, sucrose- (sugar-) free versions of no more than 300 ml.

☐ **Fresh fruit** – this is the best choice. Single pieces or fruit salad – no more than two tennis balls in size.

☐ **Fruit bars** – one dried fruit bar (maximum 40 g).

☐ **Fruit rolls** – to meet the criteria on page 72.

☐ **Health bars** – to meet the criteria on page 72.

☐ **Muffins** – one home-made low GI, low fat (see recipe in the Appendix on page 184).

☐ **Nuts or seeds** – one small handful of about 30 g.

☐ **Peanut butter** – one tablespoon with fresh apple wedges, pear or any other piece of fruit.

☐ **Popcorn** – two cups popped corn, preferably air-popped or the lower fat version.

☐ **Pretzels** – the smallest packet you can find, no more than 30 g.

☐ **Rusks or biscotti** – one or two home-made low GI, low fat (see recipe in the Appendix on page 187).

☐ **Salad** – one cup of assorted salads from a salad bar; stick to those without dressing.

☐ **Stewed dried fruit** – half a cup.

☐ **Tuna and fruit** – half an easy-to-open packet or mini tin of tuna with one fresh fruit.

☐ **Yoghurt** – one small tub flavoured or plain low-fat or fat-free yoghurt (maximum 175 ml), with berries if desired.

Suggested smart snacks.

five
PORTION DISTORTION

O ver the centuries the size of food portions has steadily increased. It is not just movie combos that have grown since the 1950s; even food portions depicted in famous paintings spanning several centuries have grown substantially over time. Most recipe book portions, takeaways and restaurant portions have become distorted and today we are bombarded not only with more choice, but also with bigger portions than we need, without even realising it. And the more we see, the more we eat.

Half a portion of quiche with a large salad (page 97).

THE BIG BALANCING ACT

All meals eaten away from home should ideally fit into the balanced meal on a plate. Try to consider the balanced meal on a plate and keep to these proportions, no matter where you are eating. This is a huge challenge and you may struggle to get it right, but do the best you can.

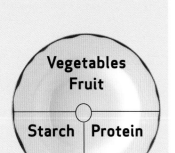

Step 1 Consider that half of what you order and eat should be salad, vegetables or fruit – colour from nature's colour palette.

Step 2 The starch (hamburger roll, pizza base, wrap, chips, etc.) should be the size of one, at the most two of your fists, and preferably low GI such as rye bread, seed loaf, sweetcorn, rice, or baby potatoes.

Step 3 The protein (chicken, hamburger patty, steak, seafood, etc.) should be limited to the size of the palm of your hand.

Step 4 Ideally no other sauce or fat should be added, as all these types of foods are already high in fat.

GUIDELINES FOR MANAGING PORTION DISTORTION

It takes only an additional 1 000 kilojoules (240 calories) a day to gain about 10 kg over a year. These 1 000 kilojoules can be found in a 50g chocolate bar, a sparsely buttered bread roll, a small kiddies milkshake, a quarter of a tramezzini or a small portion of 10 chips.

When faced with an option to supersize, be guided by your real hunger and the recommended balanced meal proportions above. You will realise as you go through the following pages that even regular portions have become distorted.

☐ Most takeaway or restaurant portions can in fact be shared between two people. Should you not be able to share, eat your meal over two sittings rather than one. For example, have half the tramezzini now and the other half a few hours later.

☐ If you wish to keep the other half of a meal for consumption later, make sure you travel with a mini cooler box with an ice brick in it to transport your meal home or back to the office. Place the leftover meal in the refrigerator as soon as you can. In this way your leftovers will still be safe for consumption within 48 hours.

☐ Eat slowly and mindfully as it takes 15 to 20 minutes for your brain to register when you are full.

☐ To prevent yourself being overly hungry when ordering food from a fast food outlet or restaurant, make sure you carry smart snacks with you at all times. See the Smart Snacking section on page 71.

☐ Preferably take your fast foods home or back to the office and serve on a dinner plate with a large salad, a generous serving of cooked vegetables or a piece of fresh fruit.

☐ Using smaller plates and glasses at home and when entertaining, makes it easier to adhere to smaller portions.

☐ Should you end up eating a larger unbalanced meal from a restaurant or takeaway, make sure you compensate for this by eating half a meal at the next meal time. Alternatively, opt for a much lighter meal such as a fresh vegetable or fruit salad or vegetable soup.

We have checked out some commonly ordered takeaway and restaurant items to show you exactly what they contain. Also included are suggestions on how to modify or combine these items with other foods to optimise nutrition. You will find items such as pizza, burgers, fried chicken, wraps, chips, tramezzinis, quiche, pasta dishes, sushi, English and health breakfasts. Snacks, such as muffins, health bars, chocolate, crisps, dried fruit, nuts and biltong as well as smoothies, milkshakes, coffees, cold drinks, fruit juices, flavoured waters and alcohol are also included.

The Build-a-meal section ends this chapter with an illustration of just how distorted nutrition can become as you add more items to a bought meal. A simple movie combo can end up providing the total energy of a day's food for a woman.

PIZZA

ONE LARGE 30 cm FOUR SEASONS PIZZA (1 PROTEIN TOPPING WITH 3 VEGETABLE TOPPINGS AND CHEESE)

ENERGY 5 718 kJ
CARBOHYDRATE 140 g
PROTEIN 72 g
FAT 61 g
SATURATED FAT 33 g
SODIUM 3 067 mg

= 4 UNBALANCED MEALS

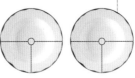

FOOD FACTS

☐ A large 30 cm pizza is equivalent to almost four high-fat meals without vegetables.

☐ Pizza bases are made from flour, a super-concentrated, refined form of carbohydrate. Thus one pizza provides the equivalent amount of starch of four meals.

☐ The protein in pizza is usually high in fat, for example cheese, salami, spare rib meat, bacon, mince, chorizo or other sausage.

☐ All the fat is found in the toppings. Choosing mostly vegetable toppings will therefore reduce the fat content. The high fat content of pizza is doubly detrimental to health as it is mostly in the saturated form.

☐ The daily sodium recommendation is 2 500 mg. One large pizza provides more sodium than what is recommended per day.

☐ To discover what happens to the nutritional value of a pizza meal when you add more toppings and extras, see Build a pizza on page 144.

SMARTER CHOICE PIZZA

TWO SLICES OF A LARGE PIZZA WITH A LARGE MIXED SALAD AND NO DRESSING

ENERGY 1 515 kJ
CARBOHYDRATE 40 g
PROTEIN 18 g
FAT 15 g
SATURATED FAT 8 g
SODIUM 766 mg

= 1 BALANCED MEAL

MEN'S CORNER
Men should have no more than three slices of pizza, provided they also include the large mixed salad without added protein and use a fat-free dressing such as lemon juice or balsamic vinegar.

OPTIMISING THE SMARTER CHOICE

☐ Two slices of pizza is the recommended serving size for women. This only provides the recommended carbohydrate, protein and fat for a healthy balanced meal, but not the vegetables. Adding a generous salad without any dressing or protein will complete the balanced meal. Order a large salad for two to share as a starter and then it will be easier to eat only two slices of pizza.

☐ Take the remaining pizza home and have one slice as the starch for your next meal. Balance this meal with a generous salad that could even contain a little dressing and some protein topping.

BURGER

ONE CHEESEBURGER WITH A SIDE ORDER OF CHIPS

ENERGY 3 268 kJ
CARBOHYDRATE 67 g
PROTEIN 34 g
FAT 41 g
SATURATED FAT 15 g
SODIUM 1 281 mg
FIBRE 3 g

= 2 UNBALANCED MEALS

FOOD FACTS

☐ One cheeseburger with only a side order of chips is equivalent to two high-fat meals without a serving of vegetables.

☐ The hamburger roll and the chips make up double the starch recommendation for a healthy meal.

☐ The fat content of this meal is almost three times the recommendation for a healthy meal.

☐ The sodium in this meal provides half of the sodium recommended for a day. This is quite acceptable as long as the other meals for the day are not also takeaway meals or high in sodium.

☐ Vegetarian burgers can contain as much fat, if not more, than meat or chicken burgers. In addition, their sodium content is often higher.

☐ Chicken fillet burgers are not necessarily a healthier option, as the chicken fillet is usually cooked with oil and larger in size than a hamburger patty. Chicken patties are as high in fat as beef patties.

☐ Ostrich burgers are the leanest of all.

SMARTER CHOICE BURGER

OPEN CHEESEBURGER WITH A LARGE TOSSED SALAD AND NO DRESSING

ENERGY 1 847 kJ
CARBOHYDRATE 22 g
PROTEIN 31 g
FAT 25 g
SATURATED FAT 10 g
SODIUM 831 mg
FIBRE 5 g

MEN'S CORNER
As men require more energy, this hamburger meal can be optimised by simply leaving out the chips and including a large salad with an oil-free dressing. Even without the chips though, this meal is strictly speaking still too high in fat for men.

= 1 BALANCED MEAL

OPTIMISING THE SMARTER CHOICE

☐ An open burger, using only half the roll and without any chips, will provide the correct amount of starch and protein. To balance the meal you still need to add vegetables.

☐ A generous salad with a fat-free dressing such as lemon juice or balsamic vinegar should be added or eaten as a starter to make a more balanced meal.

☐ Despite leaving out the chips, the fat content of this meal is 25 g, which is almost double the recommendation.

☐ Be sensible about your beverage choice and choose water or a sugar-free cold drink, rather than a milkshake, sugared cold drink, fruit juice or smoothie.

FRIED CHICKEN AND CHIPS

THREE PIECES OF FRIED CHICKEN AND A FULL PORTION OF CHIPS

ENERGY 5 033 kJ
CARBOHYDRATE 65 g
PROTEIN 70 g
FAT 73 g
SATURATED FAT 15 g
SODIUM 2 308 mg
FIBRE 6 g

= 3 UNBALANCED MEALS

FOOD FACTS

☐ Three pieces of fried chicken with a full portion of chips is equivalent to more than three meals. The energy provided by this meal, about 5 000 kJ, is the total daily energy allowance for a woman on a slimming diet.

☐ The crumb coating on the chicken pieces is equivalent to a whole slice of bread and together with the chips, the amount of starch provided is double what it should be.

☐ As chicken is a very concentrated source of protein, the protein content of this meal is more than three times the recommendation for a healthy meal.

☐ Deep-frying chicken trebles the fat content, and with the chips the fat content of this meal is five times the recommendation for a healthy meal.

☐ As with all takeaway foods, the sodium in this single meal provides all the sodium recommended for a day.

☐ Three battered chicken strips are equal to one chicken breast.

☐ A fried chicken wing and a drumstick are equivalent in nutritional value.

SMARTER CHOICE FRIED CHICKEN AND SALAD

ONE PIECE OF FRIED CHICKEN WITH A LARGE TOSSED SALAD AND NO DRESSING

ENERGY 1 631 kJ
CARBOHYDRATE 12 g
PROTEIN 39 g
FAT 21 g
SATURATED FAT 5 g
SODIUM 1 063 mg
FIBRE 2 g

= 1 BALANCED MEAL

MEN'S CORNER
Men can add either a second piece of chicken or a small side order of chips. Do not leave out the salad. The smartest choice would be to have one piece of chicken with a large salad and a serving of mash or sweet-corn.

OPTIMISING THE SMARTER CHOICE

☐ Choose one piece of chicken and to balance this meal, drop the chips and order a generous side salad with an oil-free dressing. Note that by not eating the chips, your fat consumption will be 60% less. Despite this, the fat in the meal is still above the recommendation of 15 g per meal.

☐ Coleslaw is not a good salad choice as it adds a lot more fat to an already high-fat meal.

☐ For those not watching their weight, a small serving of mash or sweetcorn can be ordered with this meal.

WRAP

ONE AVERAGE WRAP

ENERGY 2 298 kJ
CARBOHYDRATE 52 g
PROTEIN 37 g
FAT 25 g
SATURATED FAT 8 g
FIBRE 4 g
SODIUM 978 mg

= 1½ UNBALANCED MEALS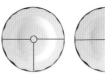

FOOD FACTS

☐ The energy content of an average wrap is equivalent to one-and-a-half meals, which means that most wraps are 50% more than we need at any one meal.

☐ Wraps are usually filled with adequate protein but minimal vegetables or salad. Usually only 5% of a wrap is vegetables.

☐ In general wraps are too big and contain too much refined, concentrated carbohydrate. Wraps should be the diameter of a side plate, rather than the size of a dinner plate.

☐ Sweet-chilli sauce, barbeque and other sauces may be fat free, but are thickened with refined starches resulting in a high carbohydrate and sugar content.

☐ The fat content of most wraps is almost double the recommendation for a healthy meal. What is more, most of the fat is the less beneficial, saturated kind.

☐ Eating a half portion of chips with a wrap adds the equivalent energy of another full meal, as well as doubling the already high fat content.

SMARTER CHOICE WRAP AND SALAD

**HALF A WRAP WITH A
LARGE TOSSED SALAD
AND NO DRESSING**

ENERGY 1 234 kJ
CARBOHYDRATE 31 g
PROTEIN 20 g
FAT 13 g
SATURATED FAT 4 g
FIBRE 4 g
SODIUM 500 mg

= 1 **BALANCED MEAL**

MEN'S CORNER
Strictly speaking, men
should have three-
quarters of a wrap
with salad served with
an oil-free dressing.
However, this is not
practical so make sure
you add a large salad
to your wrap without
any side order, crisps
or chips.

OPTIMISING THE SMARTER CHOICE

☐ To make a balanced meal of a wrap, you will need to share it with a friend or eat only half and include a large French-type salad drizzled with balsamic vinegar or lemon juice.

☐ When choosing your wrap, watch out for hidden fats in wrap fillings such as fried halloumi cheese, sausages, bacon, avocado, hummus and mayonnaise-based sauces.

☐ Ask for sauces not to be included in the wrap, but served on the side so that you can drizzle on just enough sauce to add flavour, if you choose to do so.

HOT CHIPS

FULL PORTION OF HOT CHIPS

ENERGY 3 702 kJ
CARBOHYDRATE 100 g
PROTEIN 12 g
FAT 48 g
SATURATED FAT 15 g
SODIUM 1 489 mg

= 2½ UNBALANCED MEALS

FOOD FACTS

☐ A full portion of hot chips, about three fistfuls, provides more than double the energy recommended for a light meal.

☐ Potatoes are not a vegetable. Apart from having no colour from salad or vegetables, a meal of hot chips is far too high in fat and concentrated starch.

☐ A single fistful of 10 chips or 100 g (the preferred portion for women), is actually equivalent to two starch portions and three fat portions.

☐ Potato chips are deep-fried in oil and therefore very high in fat. One full portion of hot chips in fact contains almost your daily fat allowance.

☐ Frying foods in oil that is kept hot continuously, may greatly increase the trans fatty acid content of the fried food. Trans fatty acids are implicated in many diseases.

☐ As hot chips are salted, one full portion contains three times the sodium recommendation for a healthy meal. Not ideal for those with high blood pressure.

SMARTER CHOICE HOT CHIPS AND SALAD

ONE FISTFUL OF CHIPS WITH A LARGE SALAD TOPPED WITH SOME PROTEIN AND NO DRESSING

ENERGY 1 796 kJ
CARBOHYDRATE 38 g
PROTEIN 22 g
FAT 20 g
SATURATED FAT 6 g
SODIUM 528 mg

= 1 BALANCED MEAL

MEN'S CORNER
Strictly speaking, men should follow the same advice given alongside, using their fist as a guide. For those who are active and not overweight, a full portion of chips can be eaten on rare occasions.

OPTIMISING THE SMARTER CHOICE

- ☐ Hot chips are the biggest culprit in making meals away from home unhealthy. In most cases chips are unnecessary as they only add excessive kilojoules and fat.

- ☐ To make hot chips part of a balanced meal, you need to add a large salad topped with some lean protein such as grilled chicken strips, grilled calamari, tuna in brine, low-fat cottage cheese, a boiled egg, ham, smoked salmon or trout. Serve this salad with only one fistful of chips.

- ☐ Oven chips, baked in the oven without added oil, contain half the fat of regular fried hot chips. However, the correct serving size would still be a fistful of oven chips as one medium potato would make one fistful of chips.

- ☐ Eating only a few hot chips from somebody else's plate may be equivalent to a whole starch portion with fat. Think twice before nibbling on those hot chips.

TRAMEZZINI

SPINACH AND FETA TRAMEZZINI WITH CRISPS AND SALAD

ENERGY 4 676 kJ
CARBOHYDRATE 87 g
PROTEIN 40 g
FAT 68 g
FIBRE 9 g
SODIUM 1 629 mg

= 3 UNBALANCED MEALS

FOOD FACTS

☐ One tramezzini with crisps and garnish masquerading as a salad is equivalent to three meals.

☐ Tramezzinis in general contain too much refined, concentrated carbohydrate, as the pita bread used is usually too big. The carbohydrate content is in fact double the maximum recommendation for a healthy meal.

☐ Despite this being a spinach tramezzini, the generous amounts of mozzarella cheese used in all tramezzinis together with the feta cheese, provide too much protein.

☐ Tramezzinis with chicken or meat fillings would contain more than double the amount of protein required at a meal.

☐ Tramezzinis are full of hidden fat because of the generous amounts of cheese used. Without chips, they mostly contain about four times as much fat as should be in a healthy meal.

☐ For those with high blood pressure the above tramezzini meal contains more than half of the sodium allowance for a day.

SMARTER CHOICE TRAMEZZINI AND SALAD

HALF A TRAMEZZINI WITH A LARGE SALAD AND NO DRESSING

ENERGY 1 917 kJ
CARBOHYDRATE 35 g
PROTEIN 20 g
FAT 28 g
FIBRE 5 g
SODIUM 750 mg

= 1 BALANCED MEAL

OPTIMISING THE SMARTER CHOICE

☐ Having half a tramezzini without the crisps or chips and including a large mixed salad creates a balanced main meal because it is still too high in energy and fat for a light meal.

☐ As tramezzinis are already full of cheese, which provides protein and fat, your filling choices should be as colourful as possible. Choose sun-dried tomato, spinach, rocket, peppers, mushrooms, artichokes or onion, for example.

☐ Order a tramezzini and a salad to share, so that they can be plated separately as two meals of salad with half a tramezzini each. Alternatively, ask for half your tramezzini and salad to be plated, and the other half to be put in a takeaway container. Store this in your mini cooler bag with an ice brick until you are able to refrigerate it.

QUICHE AND SALAD

QUICHE WITH SALAD AND DRESSING

ENERGY 2 790 kJ
CARBOHYDRATE 40 g
PROTEIN 17 g
FAT 50 g
SATURATED FAT 22 g
FIBRE 2 g
SODIUM 950 mg

= 2 UNBALANCED MEALS

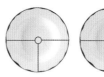

FOOD FACTS

☐ Quiches are not as healthy as people generally think. They are made with high-fat ingredients including pastry, cream, cheese, fried mushrooms, fried onions, fried bacon, and so on.

☐ The fat content is generally more than three times the maximum recommended for a healthy meal. In addition, almost half of this is made up of the less healthy saturated fats.

☐ Even if you choose a vegetable-filled quiche such as spinach quiche, the fibre content is surprisingly low and the fat content will still be too high.

☐ A regular serving of quiche and salad, with dressing, is equivalent to two meals.

☐ Commercially-made quiches also contain too much sodium.

SMARTER CHOICE QUICHE AND SALAD

HALF A QUICHE PORTION WITH A LARGE SALAD DRIZZLED WITH DRESSING

ENERGY 1 790 kJ
CARBOHYDRATE 32 g
PROTEIN 10 g
FAT 29 g
SATURATED FAT 12 g
FIBRE 3 g
SODIUM 775 mg

= 1 BALANCED MEAL

OPTIMISING THE SMARTER CHOICE

☐ To make quiche part of a balanced meal, double up the salad vegetables, halve the quiche portion and keep to two teaspoons of salad dressing.

☐ Order a quiche with an additional French-style salad to share, so that they can be plated separately as two meals of salad and half a portion of quiche each.

☐ Alternatively, ask for half your quiche to be plated with the salad, and the other half to be put in a takeaway container. Store this in your mini cooler bag with an ice brick until you are able to refrigerate it.

☐ Consuming a conservative slice of quiche and only two teaspoons of salad dressing, almost halves the fat content from 50 g to 29 g. However, the fat content of this optimised version is still double the recommendation for a healthy meal.

☐ Omitting the regular salad dressing and using balsamic vinegar or lemon juice instead would further reduce the fat content by 8 g.

☐ Adding extra salad doubles the fibre content. However, the minimum fibre content of a meal should be 5 g or more.

CURRY AND RICE

MEAT CURRY AND RICE

ENERGY 3 000 kJ
CARBOHYDRATE 72 g
PROTEIN 42 g
FAT 27 g
SATURATED FAT 10 g
FIBRE 5 g
SODIUM 1 100 mg

= 2 UNBALANCED MEALS

FOOD FACTS

☐ The challenge with takeaway curries is that they are usually too high in fat because the meat (which already contains fat) is browned in generous amounts of oil and/or butter (ghee). What is more, curries usually contain fattier cuts of meat.

☐ Most curries already contain at least one starch portion in the form of potato and thickeners. Adding one cup of rice per serving contributes a further two to three starch portions.

☐ The accompaniments eaten with curry such as poppadums, roti and naan bread will further exaggerate the refined starch and energy content.

☐ Each tablespoon of chutney contains about 100 kJ.

☐ A regular serving of curry and rice is equivalent to two high-fat meals without adequate vegetables.

☐ Half the daily sodium recommendation is found in one serving of curry and rice.

SMARTER CHOICE VEGETABLE CURRY AND SAMBALS

VEGETABLE CURRY WITH SAMBALS

ENERGY 1 634 kJ
CARBOHYDRATE 60 g
PROTEIN 7 g
FAT 15 g
SATURATED FAT 1 g
FIBRE 8 g
SODIUM 860 mg

= 1 BALANCED MEAL

MEN'S CORNER
The smartest choice for men would be one serving of vegetable curry with only half a cup of rice, plus generous portions of sambals. Alternatively, men could have a meat curry with only half a cup of rice and generous portions of sambals. This would still provide three times the recommended fat content and 30% too much energy. Compensate for this by reducing your fat intake at your next meal and snack.

OPTIMISING THE SMARTER CHOICE

☐ Choosing a vegetable curry is the smartest choice, but to ensure a balanced meal, the rice needs to be omitted and vegetable sambals added, as shown in the photograph.

☐ If you prefer a meat or chicken curry, opt for half a cup of curry with half a cup of rice. This means a single serving of takeaway curry should serve two people.

☐ To complete the meal, vegetable sambals (pictured) and salad should be added.

PASTA AND SAUCE

PASTA ALFREDO WITH PARMESAN

ENERGY 4 595 kJ
CARBOHYDRATE 97 g
PROTEIN 42 g
FAT 61 g
SATURATED FAT 35 g
FIBRE 10 g
SODIUM 883 mg

= 2½ UNBALANCED MEALS

FOOD FACTS

☐ The average plate of pasta and sauce in a restaurant contains four fistfuls of pasta. Preceding the pasta with focaccia or bread rolls can easily double the starch again. Altogether this makes for a highly refined, concentrated, unbalanced meal.

☐ Most pasta sauces contain cream and/or butter. One plate of pasta and sauce could in fact supply the total daily fat recommended for women: up to 60 g per day.

☐ Each tablespoon of grated Parmesan cheese sprinkled over the pasta adds another 3 g fat and 170 kJ.

☐ In addition, pasta meals such as spaghetti bolognaise, macaroni cheese, pasta marinara and lasagne are usually devoid of vegetables. Tomato-based sauces for pasta may provide at most one vegetable portion from the fresh tomato.

☐ Ideally a meal for a woman should contain one fistful of starch. With pasta dishes in restaurants, one can make the occasional exception and double this to two fistfuls of pasta.

SMARTER CHOICE PASTA AND SAUCE WITH SALAD

TWO FISTFULS OF PASTA WITH A TOMATO-BASED SAUCE, 2 T PARMESAN AND A LARGE SALAD

ENERGY 1 770 kJ
CARBOHYDRATE 65 g
PROTEIN 20 g
FAT 10 g
SATURATED FAT 4 g
FIBRE 6 g
SODIUM 362 mg

= 1 BALANCED MEAL

MEN'S CORNER
Always choose a plain mixed salad instead of focaccia or bread as a starter. Choose a meat, fish or chicken sauce made with tomato rather than cream. Have only half of the serving as recommended here.

OPTIMISING THE SMARTER CHOICE

☐ Since the pasta serving is always too large, it is best to share pasta meals and add a salad. When placing your order ask the waiter to serve the pasta dish on two plates. Alternatively, eat only half the dish and take the other half home for lunch or dinner the next day, remembering to add your salad.

☐ Always choose a salad instead of focaccia or bread as a starter. Remember that the salad should have no protein toppings such as cheese, calamari, chicken or tuna, and should preferably be enjoyed with an oil-free dressing.

☐ Choose tomato-based pasta sauces, which not only lower the fat content of the meal, but also add approximately one vegetable serving.

☐ The strategy with pasta dishes is therefore to minimise the pasta and maximise the vegetable and/or salad intake as suggested above.

☐ Strictly speaking, no dessert should be eaten with such a concentrated meal.

SUSHI MEAL

SUSHI COMBO PLATTER: TWO NIGIRI, EIGHT CALIFORNIA ROLLS, TWO FASHION SANDWICHES

ENERGY 2 755 kJ
CARBOHYDRATE 78 g
PROTEIN 26 g
FAT 30 g
SATURATED FAT 5 g
FIBRE 12 g
SODIUM 3 190 mg

= 2 UNBALANCED MEALS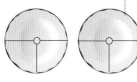

FOOD FACTS

☐ An average sushi meal of about 12 pieces is equal to almost two unbalanced meals and is not necessarily low in fat.

☐ Sushi meals are predominantly rice and protein from fish and are therefore unbalanced as the colour from nature (vegetable or salad) is missing.

☐ Sushi rolls or fashion sandwiches contain mayonnaise and/or avocado and are therefore higher in fat. Plain rice topped with fish (nigiri) will have considerably less fat compared with the sushi rolls.

☐ It is interesting to note that of the total fat, a very small percentage comes from saturated fat, which makes sushi a healthier source of fat.

☐ Sushi meals are slow release and low GI because of the soluble fibre in the seaweed, the protein and the vinegar used in the preparation of the rice.

☐ As the soya sauce is very high in sodium, those with high blood pressure or who are salt sensitive should use as little as possible.

SMARTER CHOICE SUSHI MEAL AND SALAD

SIX SUSHI PIECES: FOUR CALIFORNIA ROLLS, ONE FASHION SANDWICH AND ONE NIGIRI, WITH A LARGE SALAD

ENERGY 1 463 kJ
CARBOHYDRATE 44 g
PROTEIN 14 g
FAT 15 g
SATURATED FAT 2 g
FIBRE 6 g
SODIUM 1 595 mg

= 1 BALANCED MEAL

OPTIMISING THE SMARTER CHOICE

☐ When ordering sushi in a restaurant or buying sushi at a takeaway, choose six sushi pieces and add a large mixed salad.

☐ Most supermarkets have delicious salad bars where you can pick a variety of salads with low-oil dressings to add to your sushi meal. Remember, the salad should have no protein topping such as cheese, calamari, chicken or tuna, and should be dressed with an oil-free dressing.

☐ Because of the higher salt intake from the soya sauce, the ideal beverage with sushi would be still or sparkling unflavoured water.

MEN'S CORNER
When ordering sushi in a restaurant or buying sushi at a takeaway, choose nine sushi pieces and add a large mixed salad. Adding a generous salad is mandatory to balance the meal. The salad should have no protein topping such as cheese, calamari, chicken or tuna, as the sushi already provides enough protein. Salad dressings should be oil free.

ENGLISH BREAKFAST

ONE FULL ENGLISH BREAKFAST WITH A SMALL GLASS OF FRUIT JUICE

ENERGY 4 779 kJ
CARBOHYDRATE 61 g
PROTEIN 55 g
FAT 74 g
SATURATED FAT 27 g
FIBRE 6 g
SODIUM 2 648 mg

= 4 UNBALANCED MEALS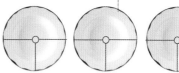

FOOD FACTS

☐ A typical English breakfast served with a small glass of fruit juice is equivalent to four unbalanced meals.

☐ The fat content of this meal is far more than what is recommended for a healthy meal: 14 fat portions, as opposed to two fat portions. Not only is everything fried, but the sausage and bacon are high-fat foods as well.

☐ This meal is dominated by protein due to the eggs, sausage and bacon. Ideally a breakfast should provide protein foods no larger than the palm of your hand. This means that you should have only one egg with either one small sausage or one rasher of bacon.

☐ Scrambled egg and omelettes are usually made with two to three eggs, which would increase the already high protein content.

☐ The two slices of toast and jam provide double the recommended carbohydrate for a breakfast. Ideally women only need one slice of toast without jam, as this provides the fistful of starch for a meal.

☐ Because of the processed meats, bacon and sausage, this is a high-sodium meal that provides the sodium recommended for a whole day.

☐ Usually coffee or tea with milk and sugar forms part of the breakfast, adding to the energy content.

SMARTER CHOICE ENGLISH BREAKFAST

= 1 BALANCED MEAL

ADJUSTED ENGLISH BREAKFAST

ENERGY 1 618 kJ
CARBOHYDRATE 24 g
PROTEIN 21 g
FAT 22 g
SATURATED FAT 5 g
FIBRE 6 g
SODIUM 643 mg

MEN'S CORNER
Follow the advice alongside. An additional portion of half a cup of baked beans can be added to the single slice of toast to make up the fistful of starch. Most men would prefer two eggs. However, adding another fried egg not only increases the protein but also brings the fat to double the recommendation. The maximum recommended fat per meal for a man is 15 g.

OPTIMISING THE SMARTER CHOICE

☐ To make a balanced meal, choose one egg and one rasher of bacon or one small sausage to fit into the palm of your hand. Double up on the tomato and add a generous portion of mushrooms to bring the vegetable content to half a plate.

☐ Only have one slice of lower GI toast without the butter and jam.

☐ As fruit juice is too concentrated, it should not be added to meals.

☐ If you are cooking an English breakfast at home, use poached eggs, grilled lean bacon, grilled tomatoes and poached mushrooms. This would reduce your fat to the recommended maximum of 15 g fat per meal and also bring the energy content into line.

HEALTH BREAKFAST

ONE HEALTH BREAKFAST: FRUIT SALAD, MUESLI, YOGHURT AND HONEY

ENERGY 2 082 kJ
CARBOHYDRATE 98 g
PROTEIN 12 g
FAT 9 g
SATURATED FAT 3 g
FIBRE 9 g
SODIUM 73 mg

= 1¹/₃ UNBALANCED MEALS

FOOD FACTS

☐ Muesli and honey are very concentrated in carbohydrate with the muesli also possibly being high in fat. Each level tablespoon of honey is equivalent to a whole starch portion.

☐ This meal usually provides only one fruit but more than five starch portions because of the concentrated honey and muesli.

☐ Muesli is a good source of fibre but portions should still be limited to 40 g or three tablespoons otherwise the carbohydrate and fat content can become excessive.

☐ Usually coffee or tea with milk and sugar and/or fruit juice would be part of the breakfast. This would add to the concentrated carbohydrate and energy content.

☐ It is interesting to note that a small restaurant English breakfast consisting of one fried egg, one rasher of bacon or one small sausage with tomato, mushrooms and one slice of unbuttered toast, provides about the same energy (kilojoules) as a regular health breakfast.

SMARTER CHOICE HEALTH BREAKFAST

ADJUSTED HEALTH BREAKFAST

ENERGY 1 574 kJ
CARBOHYDRATE 65 g
PROTEIN 12 g
FAT 9 g
SATURATED FAT 3 g
FIBRE 9 g
SODIUM 71 mg

= 1 BALANCED MEAL

MEN'S CORNER
In terms of energy, the regular health breakfast is suitable for men. However, the carbohydrate content is too high due to the concentrated honey and muesli.

OPTIMISING THE SMARTER CHOICE

- ☐ By simply omitting the honey altogether, this breakfast is balanced with the exception of the carbohydrate content, which is too high due to the concentrated muesli.
- ☐ At home, use only three tablespoons of lower fat muesli with a maximum fat content of 8 g fat per 100 g and low-fat or fat-free yoghurt.
- ☐ Add at least one tennis ball of fruit to balance the meal.

COFFEE-SHOP MUFFINS

ONE LARGE MUFFIN WITH BUTTER, JAM AND CHEESE

ENERGY 4 748 kJ
CARBOHYDRATE 152 g
PROTEIN 15 g
FAT 48 g

FOOD FACTS

☐ Most coffee-shop muffins are high-fat, refined cake under the guise of a healthy option. One muffin is in fact equivalent to approximately ten 500 kJ snacks.

☐ In addition, the fat content of one muffin is eight times that recommended for a snack.

☐ One muffin is equivalent to five slices of buttered bread and jam.

☐ The extras served on the side with muffins make up 1 000 kJ:
   • One 8 g pat of butter adds 245 kJ.
   • One mini portion of jam adds 225 kJ.
   • Three tablespoons of grated cheese add 300 kJ.

☐ It is interesting to note that a large 125 g packet of crisps contains the same amount of fat as a large coffee-shop muffin (without extras). Take a look at page 116.

SMARTER CHOICE COFFEE-SHOP MUFFINS

ONE SLICE OF A LARGE MUFFIN (WITHOUT EXTRAS)

PER SLICE OF MUFFIN:
ENERGY 940 kJ
CARBOHYDRATE 35 g
PROTEIN 2 g
FAT 10 g

MEN'S CORNER
One-quarter of a large muffin without any extras and an unsweetened beverage would be quite acceptable on the odd occasion.

OPTIMISING THE SMARTER CHOICE

☐ Ideally one-fifth of a muffin is acceptable as a special treat. In practice, however, one would probably divide a muffin into quarters.

☐ Do not add any extras as they add extra energy and fat.

☐ Beverages consumed with muffins should be unsweetened, for example regular herbal teas, coffee, water or skinny cappuccino.

SMALLER STORE-BOUGHT MUFFINS

ONE CUPCAKE-SIZE MUFFIN

ENERGY 1 583 kJ
CARBOHYDRATE 51 g
PROTEIN 5 g
FAT 16 g

FOOD FACTS

☐ Commercial muffins are highly refined and very dense. One muffin the size of a cupcake is equivalent to three snacks.

☐ Bought muffins should be used as a special treat, and not as a regular lunch-box item.

SMARTER CHOICE STORE-BOUGHT MUFFINS

HALF A CUPCAKE-SIZE MUFFIN

PER HALF MUFFIN:
ENERGY 791 kJ
CARBOHYDRATE 25 g
PROTEIN 3 g
FAT 8 g

MEN'S CORNER
One store-bought muffin can be enjoyed as an occasional snack treat. However, two home-made, healthier option muffins are suitable as a regular snack.

OPTIMISING THE SMARTER CHOICE

☐ Ideally half a store-bought muffin is the acceptable portion size for an occasional snack. By sharing the muffin with someone, you will not be tempted to eat the other half.

☐ By baking your own lower fat, lower GI healthier muffins, not only can this be a regular snack, but you can also have a whole muffin. See the bran muffin recipe on page 184.

HEALTH BARS

ONE HEALTH BAR

PER 45 g BAR:
ENERGY 826 kJ
CARBOHYDRATE 26 g
PROTEIN 4 g
FAT 8 g

FOOD FACTS

☐ Most health bars are as concentrated as chocolate. Both contain too much sugar and fat. Most health bars are in fact equal to two snacks and often contain an imbalance of nutrients. For example, breakfast and cereal bars usually contain only refined carbohydrate and too much fat.

☐ Protein bars are generally bigger than regular health bars and are therefore less suitable as a snack. Ideally, every gram of protein in a snack bar should be matched by a gram of carbohydrate. For example a bar containing 12 g protein, should contain at least 12 g carbohydrate.

SMARTER CHOICE HEALTH BARS

**HALF A HEALTH BAR
OR APPLE SLICES WITH
PEANUT BUTTER**

PER 25 g BAR:
ENERGY 460 kJ
CARBOHYDRATE 14 g
PROTEIN 2.4 g
FAT 5 g

MEN'S CORNER
One 45 g health bar
would be suitable.
However this should
not be consumed with
a soft drink or fruit
juice.

OPTIMISING THE SMARTER CHOICE

☐ The ideal portion size would be half a bar, weighing not more than 30 g. Look out for smaller sized bars to make it easier to only consume the correct amount.

☐ Larger bars should be shared. Alternatively, for those with lots of "won't power", keep the other half for another snack.

☐ Fruit-based bars are generally the better option as they contain less fat.

☐ A small apple with one level tablespoon peanut butter or Nutella would provide the same energy as half a health bar, but with better nutrition and better satiety.

CHOCOLATE BARS

ONE REGULAR CHOCOLATE BAR

PER 50 g BAR:
ENERGY 1 000 kJ
CARBOHYDRATE 28 g
PROTEIN 3.5 g
FAT 15 g

FOOD FACTS

☐ Most chocolates and chocolate bars contain 30% fat, most of which is in the less beneficial saturated form. Belgian, Swiss and other good-quality chocolate contains more fat than regular chocolate. This also applies to most sugar-free chocolates.

☐ Chocolate does not contain enough milk to be considered a source of calcium.

☐ Dark chocolate and carob have almost the same nutritional value as regular chocolate. Although dark chocolate is rich in polyphenols, the recommended 25 g portion does not provide enough polyphenols for better health.

☐ Chocolate eaten occasionally in controlled amounts can be part of a healthy lifestyle.

SMARTER CHOICE CHOCOLATE BARS

HALF A CHOCOLATE BAR OR TWO ROWS OF A 100 g SLAB

PER 25 g BAR:
ENERGY 500 kJ
CARBOHYDRATE 14 g
PROTEIN 2 g
FAT 7.5 g

MEN'S CORNER
One chocolate bar is acceptable on special occasions although strictly speaking it is not a healthy snack.

OPTIMISING THE SMARTER CHOICE

☐ Half a 50 g chocolate bar or a quarter of a 100 g slab of chocolate is suitable as an occasional snack.

☐ When eating chocolate, be mindful and fully savour the decadent flavours and texture of the chocolate.

CRISPS

ONE LARGE 125 g PACKET OF CRISPS

PER 125 g PACKET:
ENERGY 2 750 kJ
CARBOHYDRATE 62 g
PROTEIN 8 g
FAT 41 g

FOOD FACTS

☐ Savoury snacks such as crisps are not necessarily a healthier option than a sweet snack such as chocolate. Both contain almost the same amount of fat, refined carbohydrate and kilojoules per 100 g.

☐ One large 125 g packet of crisps is equivalent to four slices of buttered white bread.

☐ Even though the label on crisps may claim that they are free of trans fatty acids, this does not make them a better snack option as they are all still very high in fat.

☐ Although pretzels and flavoured popcorn may contain about half the fat of crisps, they are still very refined and concentrated snacks, providing almost the same energy (kilojoules) as crisps.

☐ All crisps, pretzels and flavoured popcorn are high in sodium and not suitable for those with high blood pressure.

SMARTER CHOICE CRISPS

ONE SMALL 25 g PACKET OF CRISPS

PER 25 g PACKET:
ENERGY 550 kJ
CARBOHYDRATE 12 g
PROTEIN 2 g
FAT 8 g

MEN'S CORNER
Men can have a 30 g packet of crisps or flavoured popcorn or 20 pretzels (40 g).

OPTIMISING THE SMARTER CHOICE

☐ A small 25 g packet of crisps or flavoured popcorn would be acceptable as an occasional treat snack.

☐ Pretzels may contain less fat than crisps and therefore the correct snack portion size can be 30 g – about 16 pretzels.

☐ Do not have crisps with dips as most dips are very high in fat.

☐ Although these snacks are considered high-sodium foods, the sodium content of crisps, pretzels and flavoured popcorn is acceptable provided the portion size is correct.

☐ Two Provitas topped with cheese would be equivalent to a small packet of crisps.

ROASTED NUTS

100 g ASSORTED ROASTED NUTS

PER 100 g ASSORTED
ROASTED AND SALTED
NUTS:
ENERGY 2 586 kJ
CARBOHYDRATE 16 g
PROTEIN 16 g
FAT 56 g

FOOD FACTS

☐ Most nuts come in 100 g packets, which is equivalent to five snacks.

☐ Roasting nuts concentrates the energy and nutrients by about 10% due to the moisture loss during the heat treatment.

☐ Since nuts and seeds contain predominantly the more beneficial unsaturated fat, they are a better fat choice. However, they are still a high-fat food and should be eaten in moderation. Nuts usually contain 50% fat, but macadamia nuts contain 74% fat.

☐ Seeds are also higher fat foods as they contain about 30% fat.

SMARTER CHOICE ROASTED NUTS

ONE SMALL HANDFUL OF ASSORTED NUTS

PER 25 g ASSORTED ROASTED AND SALTED NUTS:
ENERGY 646 kJ
CARBOHYDRATE 4 g
PROTEIN 4 g
FAT 14 g

MEN'S CORNER
Men can have a 30 g portion of nuts. This is about 20 almonds, 20 cashews or 15 pecan halves.

OPTIMISING THE SMARTER CHOICE

☐ A quarter of a 100 g packet (25 g) or a small handful would be the appropriate size. Twenty-five grams is about 15 almonds, 15 cashews or 12 pecan halves.

☐ To keep to the recommended 25 g portion, buy nuts in bulk and pre-pack at home into 25 g packets using mini resealable bags or a vacuum sealer.

☐ Although salted nuts are considered a high-sodium food, the sodium content is acceptable in this correct portion size.

BILTONG

100 g SLICED BILTONG

PER 100 g BILTONG:
ENERGY 1 172 kJ
CARBOHYDRATE 2 g
PROTEIN 44 g
FAT 10 g

FOOD FACTS

- ☐ One 100 g packet of lean biltong provides just over two high-protein snacks.
- ☐ High-protein snacks should not be eaten on a regular basis because the human body is wired for carbohydrate as its primary source of energy.
- ☐ Meat contains appreciable amounts of hidden fat and biltong is triple-concentrated meat. In addition 40% of this fat is less beneficial saturated fat.
- ☐ Biltong is high in sodium, and one 100 g packet of biltong contains almost the daily sodium recommendation.
- ☐ Dried wors is generally higher in fat than biltong.
- ☐ Game and ostrich biltong are very lean but appreciably higher in sodium.

SMARTER CHOICE BILTONG

ONE-THIRD OF A 100 g PACKET OF BILTONG

PER 33 g BILTONG:
ENERGY 387 kJ
CARBOHYDRATE 1 g
PROTEIN 15 g
FAT 3 g

MEN'S CORNER
Strictly speaking the ideal combination for a snack with biltong, would be a large fruit or four pieces of dried fruit (40 g), with one-third of a 100 g packet of biltong. Alternatively, half a 100 g packet of lean biltong can be eaten on occasion.

OPTIMISING THE SMARTER CHOICE

☐ Ideally biltong should be combined with a fruit, fresh or dried, to make a more balanced snack containing both carbohydrate and protein.

☐ A third of a 100 g packet (33 g) is the ideal portion size for biltong, combined with one small fruit or two pieces of dried fruit (20 g).

☐ Choose leaner biltong such as game biltong, ostrich biltong or lean beef biltong.

☐ Those with high blood pressure should have biltong as an occasional snack because of its higher sodium content.

DRIED FRUIT

100 g ASSORTED DRIED FRUIT

PER 100 g ASSORTED
DRIED FRUIT:
ENERGY 1 210 kJ
CARBOHYDRATE 65 g
PROTEIN 2 g
FAT 0 g

FOOD FACTS

☐ Dried fruit is fresh fruit concentrated fivefold because most of the water in the fresh fruit is lost during the drying process.

☐ For example, two dried pear halves have the same amount of carbohydrate and energy as one fresh pear, and nine strips of dried mango are equivalent to one large fresh mango.

☐ Fruit rolls are equivalent to any type of dried fruit.

☐ Sugared dried fruit has three teaspoons of sugar added per 100 g. Therefore a 30 g portion will have only one teaspoon of added sugar, which is quite acceptable.

SMARTER CHOICE DRIED FRUIT

FOUR PIECES OF DRIED FRUIT

PER 40 g:
ENERGY 484 kJ
CARBOHYDRATE 26 g
PROTEIN 1 g
FAT 0 g

MEN'S CORNER
The ideal dried fruit portion size for a man is 60 g. For example, six tablespoons of raisins, 15 dried apricot halves, seven strips of dried mango or three dried pear halves.

OPTIMISING THE SMARTER CHOICE

☐ Fresh fruit is the best choice because it is more satisfying and nutritious. Small quantities of dried fruit should only be eaten when fresh fruit is not available or practical.

☐ The ideal portion for dried fruit and fruit rolls as a snack is 40 g. For example, four tablespoons of raisins, 10 dried apricot halves, five strips of dried mango or two dried pear halves.

☐ The ideal portion for sugared fruit dainties and sugared fruit rolls would be 30 g.

SMOOTHIES

ONE LARGE COMMERCIAL SMOOTHIE

PER 650 ml:
ENERGY 1 865 kJ
CARBOHYDRATE 93 g
PROTEIN 5 g
FAT 5 g

FOOD FACTS

As a snack:

☐ Most large smoothies are about 650 ml and equivalent to almost four snacks.

☐ Smoothies are very concentrated as they often contain too many fruits, added fruit juice, honey, sugar or flavoured syrups.

As a meal:

☐ Although a large smoothie will provide vitamins and adequate kilojoules, it is not a balanced meal because it is so concentrated in carbohydrate.

☐ A smoothie as a balanced meal should contain 200 ml milk or yoghurt per two tennis balls of fruit to ensure a good balance between carbohydrate and protein. See the Smoothies section in the Breakfasts chapter on page 39.

☐ Some smoothies are made using powder concentrates, and do not actually contain any fruit. They thus contain mostly sugar and flavouring.

SMARTER CHOICE SMOOTHIES

ONE MEDIUM SMOOTHIE

PER 500 ml MEAL:
ENERGY 1 435 kJ
CARBOHYDRATE 71 g
PROTEIN 4 g
FAT 4 g

PER 175 ml SNACK:
ENERGY 502 kJ
CARBOHYDRATE 25 g
PROTEIN 1 g
FAT 1 g

MEN'S CORNER
The same advice applies to men who wish to drink a smoothie as a meal or snack.

OPTIMISING THE SMARTER CHOICE

☐ As a snack, the ideal size for a smoothie is 175 ml, the size of a single-serve yoghurt. This means sharing a kiddies or small smoothie or, ideally, making your own.

☐ A bought medium smoothie (500 ml) can on occasion be used as a meal replacement provided a smart snack is available. This will help to prevent a drop in blood sugar two to three hours later due to the low protein in the smoothie.

☐ When making your own smoothies as a meal, each smoothie should contain no more than two tennis balls of fruit. To make your own balanced smoothie, see the Smoothies section in the Breakfasts chapter on page 39.

MILKSHAKES

ONE REGULAR MILKSHAKE

PER 400 ml:
ENERGY 2 591 kJ
CARBOHYDRATE 60 g
PROTEIN 13 g
FAT 36 g

FOOD FACTS

☐ Most milkshakes contain about 12 teaspoons of sugar due to the syrup flavouring and ice cream, whereas the sugar recommendation for a snack is no more than two teaspoons per snack.

☐ One regular milkshake contains a whole bowl of ice cream, making it a very concentrated drink that should not be consumed with a meal. In fact, the milkshake itself is equivalent to almost two unbalanced meals.

☐ Milkshakes are not only too high in sugar, but also contain six times the amount of fat that should be in a snack. In addition two-thirds of this fat is in the less beneficial saturated form.

SMARTER CHOICE MILKSHAKES

100 ml MILKSHAKE

PER 100 ml:
ENERGY 648 kJ
CARBOHYDRATE 15 g
PROTEIN 3 g
FAT 9 g

MEN'S CORNER
Milkshakes are a luxury and therefore the same advice applies to men.

OPTIMISING THE SMARTER CHOICE

☐ Strictly speaking only a quarter of a regular milkshake should be consumed as a snack. On a practical level however, order a kiddies-size milkshake with two straws and share as a snack for two people.

☐ Milkshakes should never be consumed as a beverage with a meal, although half a kiddies milkshake could serve as an occasional dessert.

SOFT DRINKS AND SPORTS DRINKS

ONE REGULAR CAN OF SOFT DRINK OR ONE BOTTLE OF A SPORTS DRINK

PER 330 ml CAN OR
500 ml SPORTS DRINK:
ENERGY 570 kJ
CARBOHYDRATE 35 g
PROTEIN 0 g
FAT 0 g

FOOD FACTS

☐ A can of soft drink or a bottle of sports drink contains about eight teaspoons of sugar, which is the sugar recommended for an entire day.

☐ Soft drinks that have been artificially sweetened contain about four tablets or two sachets of sweetener, and should be drunk in limited amounts as we recommend that no more than 10 tablets or five sachets of sweetener should be consumed per day.

☐ Soft drinks should not be consumed by children as there may be a link between compromised bone and dental health and regular soft drink consumption.

☐ Sports drinks are not meant to be used as a regular thirst quencher. They are designed for those participating in sport for longer than 90 minutes and are fast release to efficiently replenish muscle energy stores and electrolytes.

SMARTER CHOICE SOFT DRINKS AND SPORTS DRINKS

ONE SLIM CAN OF SOFT DRINK (200 ml)

PER 200 ml:
ENERGY 334 kJ
CARBOHYDRATE 21 g
PROTEIN 0 g
FAT 0 g

MEN'S CORNER
Water is still the best choice as a thirst quencher. All soft drinks are luxuries and therefore the same advice applies to men.

OPTIMISING THE SMARTER CHOICE

☐ The ideal thirst quencher is water.

☐ Should you wish to drink a soft drink, then choose a sugar-free one or the smaller 200 ml slim can.

☐ Alternatively, share a 330 ml can of soft drink, or pour about 200 ml soft drink from a large bottle into a glass with lots of ice to fill the glass.

☐ Remember that the soft drink should replace the starch of the meal you are having it with.

☐ Sports drinks should only be consumed during and after at least 90 minutes of moderate physical activity.

FLAVOURED WATER AND ICED TEA

ONE BOTTLE FLAVOURED WATER (500 ml)

PER 500 ml FLAVOURED WATER:
ENERGY 392 kJ
CARBOHYDRATE 23 g
PROTEIN 0 g
FAT 0 g

FOOD FACTS

☐ Although flavoured waters and iced teas contain fewer kilojoules than soft drinks, they are in fact soft drinks without the intense colour. They are not the same as plain water.

☐ Flavoured water or iced tea that has been artificially sweetened contains about two tablets or one sachet of sweetener, and should be drunk in limited amounts. Other drinks and snacks that are artificially sweetened also contribute to the total sweetener intake, which should be no more than 10 tablets or five sachets of sweetener per day.

☐ Since a bottle of regular flavoured water is equivalent to a slice of white bread, remember to leave out the starch at the meal at which you are having the flavoured water.

SMARTER CHOICE FLAVOURED WATER AND ICED TEA

ONE BOTTLE LITE FLAVOURED WATER

PER 500 ml LITE
FLAVOURED WATER:
ENERGY 53 kJ
CARBOHYDRATE 4 g
PROTEIN 0 g
FAT 0 g

MEN'S CORNER
Like soft drinks, flavoured waters are luxuries and therefore the same advice applies. As snacks for men can be slightly larger, a flavoured water can be added to one of the recommended snacks in the Smart Snacking section on page 77.

OPTIMISING THE SMARTER CHOICE

☐ Choosing a lite flavoured water would be the smarter choice.

☐ Snacks should contain about 500 kJ, which means that having a regular flavoured water as a snack, only allows the addition of a fruit. All other snacks are too high in kilojoules to be added to a flavoured water.

However, a lite flavoured water or lite iced tea may be combined with a recommended snack. See the Smart Snacking section on page 77.

FRUIT JUICE

ONE LARGE GLASS OF FRUIT JUICE

PER 350 ml:
ENERGY 734 kJ
CARBOHYDRATE 43 g
PROTEIN 2 g
FAT 0 g

FOOD FACTS

☐ One fruit yields about 100 ml of fruit juice, which means a large glass of fruit juice can be equivalent to four whole fresh fruit. Fruit juices are concentrated liquid fruit, without the fibre.

☐ The glycemic load of a large glass of fruit juice is that of a large meal, requiring as much insulin as a meal would. This goes to show just how concentrated fruit juices are. (For more information on the glycemic load, turn to page 74.)

☐ The above applies to fruit juices without added sugar. Those with added sugar or fructose would be even more concentrated.

☐ Grapetiser, Peartiser, Appletiser and other sparkling fruit juices are similar to regular fruit juices.

SMARTER CHOICE FRUIT JUICE

ONE SMALL GLASS OF FRUIT JUICE

PER 125 ml:
ENERGY 262 kJ
CARBOHYDRATE 15 g
PROTEIN 0.6 g
FAT 0 g

MEN'S CORNER
As the glycemic load of fruit juice is so high, it is better for men to follow the same advice given alongside.

OPTIMISING THE SMARTER CHOICE

☐ Half a glass, 125 ml, is the correct serving size for fruit juice. However, the 200 ml serving size cartons or bottles would be the most practical option.

☐ Fruit juices should always be diluted with an equal amount of still or sparkling water. Alternatively, make an iced tea by diluting fruit juice with an equal amount of any herbal tea.

☐ The equivalent amount of fresh fruit (one tennis ball of fruit) is far more satisfying and suitable as a snack.

☐ Fruit juice is not a thirst quencher, as water is.

☐ Even when diluted, fruit juice should be served in smaller glasses.

COFFEES

ONE LATTE OR MEGA CAPPUCCINO

ENERGY 944 kJ
CARBOHYDRATE 25 g
PROTEIN 12 g
FAT 8 g

FOOD FACTS

☐ Cappuccinos, lattes, hot chocolates and chai teas are not free extras but are usually equivalent to two snacks as they contain almost 1 000 kilojoules.

☐ Flavoured lattes and coffees contain extra syrup, which can double the amount of sugar and kilojoules. Honey is more concentrated than sugar and, added to coffee and tea, can easily add another 50% more energy to the drink.

☐ The caffeine content of small coffees is quite acceptable. However, supersizing or choosing the larger options can raise the caffeine content to unacceptable levels, particularly if you have more than one per day.

☐ Adding a muffin as small as a cupcake would provide an additional three starches and three fat portions. This together with a latte or mega cappuccino is equivalent to a large meal.

SMARTER CHOICE COFFEES

ONE SMALL CAPPUCCINO

ENERGY 325 kJ
CARBOHYDRATE 10 g
PROTEIN 4 g
FAT 2 g

MEN'S CORNER
Although men can, in theory, have almost double what is recommended for women, it would be better practice to choose the smaller servings.

OPTIMISING THE SMARTER CHOICE

☐ Choose the small size with an optional sachet or stick of sugar. One sachet or teaspoon of sugar adds only another 66 kilojoules, which is acceptable as long as you consume no more than three cups of tea and coffee with one teaspoon of sugar in each, per day.

☐ One artificial sweetener sachet or stick may be used instead of sugar.

☐ By asking for all milky drinks to be the "skinny" version (using fat-free or skimmed milk and no cream), the energy content can be halved.

☐ Should you be concerned about the caffeine content of coffees, choose the decaffeinated option or alternatives such as rooibos, Red Espresso or herbal teas.

BEER

SIX-PACK OF BEER

PER 6 x 330 ml:
ENERGY 3 134 kJ
CARBOHYDRATE 27 g
PROTEIN 0 g
FAT 0 g

FOOD FACTS

☐ The carbohydrate in beer contributes about 20% of the total energy, with the rest of the energy coming from the alcohol in the beer. It is therefore the alcohol, and not the carbohydrate, that taxes the liver and results in weight gain from the excess energy. Alcohol is more energy dense than carbohydrate.

☐ Alcohol is a toxin that is metabolised by the liver in preference to other liver functions. The alcohol in each drink can take two to three hours to be metabolised. However, the liver can comfortably metabolise two drinks per day in most people, not six or more.

☐ Each beer is equivalent to 1½ slices of white bread, and therefore a six-pack would be equivalent to nine slices of bread.

☐ Lite beers contain up to 30% fewer kilojoules than regular beer, and not 50% less energy, as is often implied.

SMARTER CHOICE BEER

ONE BOTTLE OF BEER

PER 330 ml:
ENERGY 522 kJ
CARBOHYDRATE 5 g
PROTEIN 0 g
FAT 0 g

MEN'S CORNER
Ideally, men should adhere to the advice given alongside, but since men tend to drink more beer, switching to lite beer would be the better option.

OPTIMISING THE SMARTER CHOICE

- ☐ Strictly speaking, one beer is the correct serving size as it is a non-essential and is usually consumed over and above other foods.
- ☐ When having a beer, compensate for the extra energy by having little or no starch with your (next) meal, since each beer is equivalent to 1½ slices of bread.
- ☐ Beer can be diluted with a sugar-free mixer to yield two beer shandies.
- ☐ Beer-drinking occasions often go hand in hand with mindless snacking on high-fat concentrated foods such as crisps, biltong, mini pastries, braaied meat, and so on. Be more mindful and try not to overindulge in such foods.
- ☐ Although a lite beer would be the best choice, the same recommendations as above apply.

WINE

ONE GLASS OF WINE

PER 200 ml:
ENERGY 596 kJ
CARBOHYDRATE 3 g
PROTEIN 0 g
FAT 0 g

FOOD FACTS

☐ A large glass of wine is equivalent to almost two slices of white bread.

☐ All types of wine are similar in that the difference in sugar is at most two grams of sugar per large glass of wine, and the alcohol content is about the same.

☐ Lite wines may contain less alcohol and/or energy, but the difference is usually too small to make an impact on total daily energy intakes.

☐ Since wine contains more alcohol than beer, one 200 ml glass of wine contains about the same amount of alcohol as a 330 ml beer.

☐ A glass of red wine contains cardio-protective compounds and may be the better choice of wine.

SMARTER CHOICE WINE

ONE SMALL GLASS OF WINE

PER 125 ml:
ENERGY 373 kJ
CARBOHYDRATE 2 g
PROTEIN 0 g
FAT 0 g

MEN'S CORNER
Although men can, in theory, have more to drink than women, they should have no more than two small glasses or one large glass of wine.

OPTIMISING THE SMARTER CHOICE

☐ Strictly speaking a bottle of wine should serve six, and not four, making the serving size 125 ml and not 200 ml.

☐ Wine can be diluted to make a spritzer using a sugar-free mixer or soda water, making two drinks instead of one. Alternatively, keep adding lots of ice to your glass instead of more wine.

☐ When drinking wine, compensate for the extra kilojoules by having no starch or pudding with your (next) meal.

☐ If you choose a lite wine, be careful not to drink more than you would if you were drinking regular wine.

COCKTAILS, COOLERS AND CIDERS

LONG ISLAND ICED TEA

PER 350 ml
ENERGY 1 200 kJ
CARBOHYDRATE 20 g
PROTEIN 0 g
FAT 0 g

FOOD FACTS

☐ One cocktail should be regarded as an occasional special treat. A tall cocktail made with three tots of alcohol and topped with fruit juice or other mixers can contain over 1 000 kJ. This equates to a whole pudding serving.

☐ Smaller Martini-like cocktails may contain one tot less alcohol and less or no mixer, but they are generally consumed faster and the temptation is to have another.

☐ Ciders, coolers and flavoured alcoholic beverages are more energy dense than beer and are more like cocktails as they contain on average 800 kilojoules.

SMARTER CHOICE COCKTAILS, COOLERS AND CIDERS

ONE SINGLE TOT WITH A SUGAR-FREE MIXER

PER DRINK:
ENERGY 300 kJ
CARBOHYDRATE 0 g
PROTEIN 0 g
FAT 0 g

MEN'S CORNER
Ideally, men should adhere to the advice given here, but since men tend to drink more, the best option would be the single tot with a sugar-free mixer.

OPTIMISING THE SMARTER CHOICE

☐ As cocktails are "pudding in a glass" the wise choice is to have one as an occasional treat.

☐ A better alternative to a cocktail is to have a drink containing a single tot of alcohol with a sugar-free mixer such as brandy and sugar-free cola or gin and sugar-free tonic water.

☐ For every cocktail or alcoholic drink, make sure you have an equal amount of water.

☐ Coolers are best poured over generous amounts of ice to dilute them and make the drink last longer.

☐ Compensate for alcoholic beverages with meals by having little or no starch with the meal, and no dessert.

SPIRITS

DOUBLE BRANDY AND COLA

PER DRINK:
ENERGY 930 kJ
CARBOHYDRATE 20 g
PROTEIN 0 g
FAT 0 g

FOOD FACTS

☐ Every tot of alcohol and every small can of mixer contains about 300 kilojoules. A double tot of alcohol with a mixer contains almost as much energy as a regular tall cocktail.

☐ An extra tot or small glass of wine every day, providing 300 kJ, can result in weight gain of about three kilograms per year, which means weight gain of 30 kg in 10 years.

☐ Alcohol is a toxin that is metabolised by the liver in preference to other liver functions. One tot of alcohol can take two to three hours to be metabolised. However, the liver can comfortably metabolise two drinks per day in most people.

SMARTER CHOICE SPIRITS

ONE SINGLE TOT OVER LOTS OF ICE

PER DRINK:
ENERGY 300 kJ
CARBOHYDRATE 0 g
PROTEIN 0 g
FAT 0 g

MEN'S CORNER
Men should adhere to the advice given alongside.

OPTIMISING THE SMARTER CHOICE

- ☐ Ideally a drink containing a single tot of alcohol with lots of ice and/or a sugar-free mixer is recommended.
- ☐ For every alcoholic drink, make sure you have an equal amount of water.
- ☐ Because of the potential for weight gain, remember to compensate for the extra energy in the alcohol by having very little or no starch with your meal.
- ☐ It is better to have one drink regularly than "saving" drinks and having a whole lot at a single occasion (binge drinking).

BUILD A MEAL

BUILD A PIZZA

BASIC PIZZA (TOMATO, CHEESE AND HERBS)

Energy 4 928 kJ   Carbohydrate 140 g   Protein 64 g   Fat 43 g

Food facts

☐ This pizza is equivalent to three unbalanced meals, and is similar to eating eight slices of bread with cheese and tomato.

☐ Even though lower fat mozzarella cheese is used on pizzas, because of the generous amounts used, the fat increases by 40 g fat per pizza.

HAM AND MUSHROOM PIZZA

Energy 5 151 kJ   Carbohydrate 141 g   Protein 74 g   Fat 44 g

Food fact

☐ Adding any vegetable topping such as mushrooms, asparagus, Peppadews, peppers, onion, fresh tomato, pineapple, spinach or artichoke has a very small impact on the energy and fat content of a pizza.

EXTRA-MEATY PIZZA

Energy 6 512 kJ   Carbohydrate 164 g   Protein 97 g   Fat 67 g

Food facts

☐ This pizza is in fact equivalent to four unbalanced meals.

☐ Adding meat toppings not only adds protein but lots of extra fat, half of which
is usually the less healthy, saturated kind.

DOUBLE-CHEESE PIZZA

Energy 8 632 kJ   Carbohydrate 168 g   Protein 132 g   Fat 107 g

Food facts

☐ Adding extra cheese, even a lower fat cheese such as mozzarella (22% fat
compared with most hard cheeses at 33% fat), significantly increases the fat
content, of which half is less healthy saturated fat.

☐ Sharing this pizza among four people gives each person a full meal that is still
lacking in vegetables.

DOUBLE-DECKER PIZZA

Energy 11 440 kJ   Carbohydrate 304 g   Protein 161 g   Fat 110 g

Food facts

☐ One double-decker pizza is equivalent to 7½ unbalanced meals.

☐ Adding the extra layer of pizza base is like adding another eight slices of bread (eight starch portions) and almost doubles the refined concentrated carbohydrate content.

☐ Just one slice (one-eighth) of a double-decker pizza is already equivalent to a whole meal, although it is totally lacking in vegetables.

TRIPLE-DECKER PIZZA

Energy 13 904 kJ   Carbohydrate 374 g   Protein 193 g   Fat 125 g

Food facts

☐ One triple-decker pizza is equivalent to nine unbalanced meals.

☐ Each slice (one-eighth) contains 16 g of fat, which is the total fat recommended for a whole meal.

☐ Need we say more?

BUILD A BURGER

BASIC BURGER

Energy 2 045 kJ   Carbohydrate 43 g   Protein 32 g   Fat 21 g

Food fact

☐ A basic hamburger is equivalent in energy to a whole meal, although it is totally lacking in vegetables. The tomato, lettuce and gherkins make up only 10% of a vegetable serving.

BASIC BURGER AND CHIPS

Energy 3 300 kJ   Carbohydrate 78 g   Protein 35 g   Fat 37 g

Food fact

☐ Adding chips adds no nutritional value, only unnecessary fat and kilojoules, and the vegetables are still missing.

DOUBLE CHEESEBURGER AND CHIPS

Energy 5 162 kJ   Carbohydrate 78 g   Protein 70 g   Fat 70 g

Food facts
☐ Doubling up on the protein almost doubles the fat content as well.
☐ A double cheeseburger and chips provides almost the total energy a
  woman should consume per day when trying to lose weight.

DOUBLE CHEESEBURGER, CHIPS AND COLA

Energy 6 000 kJ   Carbohydrate 130 g   Protein 70 g   Fat 70 g

Food fact
☐ Adding a 500 ml soft drink adds 12 teaspoons of sugar.

BUILD A BREAKFAST

BASIC BREAKFAST

Energy 1 355 kJ   Carbohydrate 34 g   Protein 11 g   Fat 16 g

Food facts
☐ This basic breakfast is a reasonably balanced meal although it would be better if the fruit juice were replaced with fresh fruit.
☐ Egg on toast is equivalent to a serving of cereal and milk.

DOUBLE BASIC BREAKFAST PLUS BACON, TOMATO AND MUSHROOMS

Energy 3 270 kJ   Carbohydrate 55 g   Protein 38 g   Fat 54 g

Food facts
☐ Although the energy content has more than doubled, the contribution from the tomato and mushrooms is negligible. They merely add necessary nutrients, without many kilojoules.
☐ This breakfast is equivalent to two unbalanced light meals with almost the full daily fat allowance.

DOUBLE BASIC BREAKFAST PLUS BACON, TOMATO, MUSHROOMS, PORK SAUSAGES AND CHIPS

Energy 5 986 kJ   Carbohydrate 89 g   Protein 61 g   Fat 90 g

Food fact

☐ This meal is equivalent to the daily energy intake for a woman, although this is not the worst concern. It is the extremely high fat content that is the real problem, as it will increase the risk of disease and encourage weight gain.

DOUBLE BASIC BREAKFAST PLUS BACON, TOMATO, MUSHROOMS, PORK SAUSAGE, CHIPS, PASTRY AND COFFEE

Energy 8 138 kJ   Carbohydrate 158 g   Protein 77g   Fat 109 g

Food facts

☐ Finishing off a sumptuous breakfast with pastry and coffee adds insult to injury. This meal is in fact equivalent to the daily energy intake for a man with an overdose of fat.

☐ Croissants, Danish pastries and muffins contain lots of fat.

BUILD A SALAD

BASIC SALAD – FRENCH STYLE, NO DRESSING

Energy 300 kJ   Carbohydrate 14 g   Protein 2 g   Fat 0.6 g

Food fact

☐ A large salad (two to three cupfuls) provides a mere 300 kilojoules with generous amounts of vitamins, minerals, phyto-nutrients and antioxidants, and makes an ideal vegetable serving for any meal.

GREEK SALAD, NO DRESSING

Energy 1 752 kJ   Carbohydrate 15 g   Protein 16 g   Fat 33 g

Food fact

☐ The feta cheese provides enough protein to make an almost balanced meal, which is lacking in a little carbohydrate, but contains twice the fat recommendation.

CHICKEN AND AVOCADO SALAD, NO DRESSING

Energy 3 162 kJ   Carbohydrate 15 g   Protein 52 g   Fat 53 g

Food facts
- ☐ This salad represents all those salads with protein toppings such as salmon, halloumi, coronation chicken, beef, calamari, and so on.
- ☐ Crumbed or fried protein increases the fat content of a salad by at least 25%.
- ☐ The salad vegetables are not the problem. It is the toppings that add all the fat, protein and excess kilojoules.

CHICKEN AND AVOCADO SALAD, WITH DRESSING

Energy 4 035 kJ   Carbohydrate 24 g   Protein 53 g   Fat 73 g

Food facts
- ☐ Think twice about adding salad dressing, as most are concentrated sources of fat. A restaurant serving of salad dressing can add up to 1 000 kilojoules.
- ☐ Although all salads are perceived as being healthy, those with generous (protein) toppings and dressing can be equivalent to a restaurant main meal.

BUILD A MOVIE COMBO

KIDDIES COMBO

Energy 1 345 kJ   Carbohydrate 53 g   Protein 3 g   Fat 12 g

Food facts

☐ The kiddies combo is in fact equivalent to two generous snacks for a woman. The ideal would be to have only the kiddies-size popcorn with a sugar-free soft drink or, better still, water.

☐ The kiddies amount of popcorn is equal to one starch and two fats, which means the supper preceding or following the movie should contain no starch or fat. Our suggestion is that supper should be a salad with a lean protein topping or a vegetable soup.

SMALL COMBO

	Energy	Carbohydrate	Protein	Fat
Popcorn and drink (500 ml):	2 135 kJ	81 g	5 g	20 g
With sweet (40 g):	2 681 kJ	112 g	8.5 g	20 g
With chocolate (45 g):	3 080 kJ	109 g	9 g	32 g

Food facts

☐ The basic popcorn and drink is equivalent to four snacks for a woman.

☐ From the soft drink alone, you get 12 teaspoons of sugar. Rather choose a sugar-free soft drink or, better still, water.

☐ Occasionally and as a special treat the popcorn and soft drink combo, without the chocolate or sweets, may replace a main meal. But only occasionally.

MEDIUM COMBO

	Energy	Carbohydrate	Protein	Fat
Popcorn and drink (650 ml):	2 926 kJ	108 g	7 g	29 g
With sweet (80 g):	4 139 kJ	180 g	7 g	27 g
With chocolate (50 g):	3 889 kJ	145 g	9 g	38 g

Food facts
☐ Even if this combo is shared between two adults, each person will still be consuming the energy equivalent of a whole meal.

☐ Whether you add fat-free sweets or chocolate, the energy added is almost identical.

☐ The soft drink and chocolate or sweets contribute at least 24 teaspoons of sugar. A healthy sugar intake is not more than two teaspoons per meal or snack.

LARGE COMBO

	Energy	Carbohydrate	Protein	Fat
Popcorn and drink (945 ml):	4 278 kJ	158 g	11 g	42 g
With sweet (125 g):	5 984 kJ	255 g	11-21 g	42 g
With chocolate (100 g):	6 609 kJ	217 g	17 g	74 g

Food facts

☐ The large combo with chocolate or sweets provides the total energy required per day for a woman without providing nutritional balance!

☐ Even if two adults shared this combo, it would still provide far too much unbalanced energy.

☐ Never choose the large combo.

six
GRAB-A-BASKET

This chapter is not about perfect nutrition but rather an attempt to address the reality that many of us do not have the time or know-how to plan and prepare healthy meals for the workplace. The concept underlying Grab-a-Basket is to shop smartly once a week for specific, planned healthy assembled meals and snacks for one person, for that work week.

The menus are based on the balanced meal principles as discussed in this book. Each meal therefore consists of a lot of colour in the form of vegetables, salad or fruit, a fistful of slow-release starch, at most a palm-sized piece of protein, and a little fat.

Basket 1. (Details on pages 164 and 165.)

HOW TO ASSEMBLE BALANCED BREAKFASTS AND LUNCHES AT WORK

Step 1 Half your plate should be filled with colour from nature's colour palette in the form of fruit or vegetables.

Step 2 Include one fistful of starch in the form of low-GI crackers, bread, mini pitas, cereals, sweetcorn, chickpeas, etc.

Step 3 Add a protein which is at most the size of the palm of your hand. For example, low-fat dairy, tuna, chicken breast, lean cold meat or boiled egg.

Step 4 Add a small portion of healthy fat such as a little low-oil salad dressing, a small handful of nuts or seeds, olives or avocado.

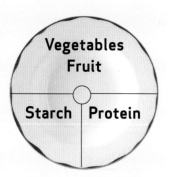

Men's corner

Men can double up either the starch or the protein for the suggested breakfasts and lunches. An extra fruit or two can also be added to any day.

All the suggested meals and snacks meet the criteria set out in the chapters on meals and snacks. (See page 29, page 47 and page 71.)

Nutrient criteria used per meal:
☐ 1 500-1 800 kJ
☐ 10-15 g fat
☐ 45 g carbohydrate
☐ less than 25 g protein

We have put together three weekly shopping baskets with matching quick-to-prepare assembled menus for breakfasts, lunches and two snacks for five days each for one person. The idea is to take the entire contents of the shopping basket to your workplace on Monday morning so that you have all your meals and snacks on hand at work.

For those on the road, or unable to store the food at their workplace, we suggest assembling each day's meals and snacks the night before and taking these along in a cooler bag.

We have assumed you have access to the following:
- ☐ Fridge space
- ☐ Basic crockery and cutlery
- ☐ Microwave
- ☐ Toaster

As we have tried to use up all the ingredients in the basket by the end of that week, particularly the perishables, this has put some constraints on variety. For example, when there is smoked salmon or trout on the menu, it is used up in two meals within one day, and cooked beetroot would be part of two different salads within the same week. Some of the non-perishable items such as oats, dressings, relish and crackers will not be used up in one week and can be used the following week.

WHAT TO DO WITH THE LEFTOVERS
- ☐ Slices of bread or mini pitas can be frozen for use at home or used as the starch for meals in the next week.
- ☐ Remaining oats and Provitas can be taken home or left at work for another week.
- ☐ Condiments and sauces are non-perishables and can be used over several weeks.
- ☐ Sealed extra cheese portions can also be kept in the fridge for several weeks.
- ☐ Leftover fruit can be taken home or shared with colleagues.
- ☐ All leftover milk can be used in tea and coffee.

READY-MADE "MEALS"

We have not included any ready-made cooked meals, not because they are not suitable, but because they differ so hugely. Many are too big, others provide too much or no starch, some are far too high in protein and fat, and the majority do not contain enough colour in the form of vegetables or salad.

If you would prefer to have a ready-made meal, consider the following:

☐ Choose meals that are no larger than 250 g per serving.

☐ To balance the ready-made meal, add at least two fistfuls of vegetables or salad.

☐ Check the nutritional analysis provided, making sure that the values are per serving. Remember to look at the "per serving" values and not the "per 100 g" ones.

Meals for women

☐ 1 500-1 800 kJ
☐ 10-15 g fat
☐ 45 g carbohydrate
☐ Less than 25 g protein
☐ Preferably 5 g fibre

Meals for men

☐ 1 800-2 200 kJ
☐ 10-15 g fat
☐ 60 g carbohydrate
☐ About 25 g protein
☐ Preferably 5 g fibre

A ready-made meal balanced with a generous salad.

BASKET ONE

FRUIT AND VEGETABLES

Apples, pack of 4
Baby carrots, 1 x packet (250 g)
Bananas or grapes, 6 kids bananas or 2 x punnets grapes (300 g each)
Beetroot, cooked, 1 x tub (400 g)
Cherry tomatoes, 2 x small punnets
Coriander, 1 x small packet (30 g)
Fruit salad or fruit chunks, 1 x 150 g single serve
Midi cucumber, 1 (the size of half an English cucumber)
Pears, pack of 4
Rocket, 1 x small punnet (30 g)
Snap peas or mange touts, 1 x tray (120 g)

STARCHES

Men: You have the option of doubling the starch or the protein in your
    meals. If you choose to double the starch, then choose the amounts in
    bold below.

Chickpeas, 1 x tin (410 g)	**(2 x tins)**
Falafel, 12 (150 g)	**(24 falafels – 300 g)**
Oats, 1 x box (500 g or smaller)	
Provitas, 1 x box with individual packs of 4	
Rye bread, 1 x packet (8 slices)	
Snack bar, 1 x small (500 kJ; 6 g fat –	
see snack criteria in Appendix)	**(750 kJ; 8 g fat)**

PROTEIN AND DAIRY

Men: You have the option of doubling the starch or the protein in your
    meals. If you choose to double the protein, then choose the amounts
    in **bold** below.

Camembert or brie cheese, 1 x round	
or wedge (125 g)	**(2 cheeses – 250 g)**

Chicken strips, cooked, 200 g   **(400 g chicken strips)**
Cottage cheese, 1 x tub (200-250 g)   **(2 x tubs – 500 g)**
Greek yoghurt, 1 x tub (175 ml)
Milk, low fat, 1% or skimmed, 1 L
Smoked trout or salmon or smoked beef,
   1 x packet (100 g)   **(200 g)**
Tuna in brine, 1 x sachet (85 g)   **(2 x sachets or 1 tin)**
Yoghurt, pear or apricot, low fat, 1 x small tub (100-150 ml)

FATS
Avocado, 1 large
Low-oil salad dressing, 1 x small bottle
Mixed nuts, 1 x packet (100 g)

EXTRAS
Lemon juice, 1 x small bottle or 1 fresh lemon
Mini jar of cheese relish or preserve or sweet-chilli sauce,
   1 x small jar or bottle
Black pepper mill
Salt mill

OPTIONAL EXTRAS (can be added to any meal)
Artichokes in brine
Asparagus spears
Fresh herbs
Gherkins
Mushrooms in brine
Peppadews
Pickled onions
Sprouts
Vinegar, balsamic or other

MONDAY

Breakfast RYE TOASTIE

1 Cut 1 **apple** into quarters and slice 2 quarters onto **rye bread**.
2 Slice ½ round or wedge of **cheese** on top of the apple slices.
3 Top with 1 tablespoon **relish** or **sweet-chilli sauce**.
4 Grill for just under a minute or microwave to melt the cheese.
5 Eat the remaining apple half while preparing the toastie.

Snack 1 **banana** or a handful of **grapes** (about 100 g) with 1 tablespoon of mixed **nuts**.

Lunch CHICKPEA, CORIANDER AND CHICKEN SALAD
(pictured)

1 Place the following in a bowl: ⅓ tin drained **chickpeas**; ½ tub cooked **beetroot**, quartered; handful of julienned **snap peas**; ¼ **avocado**, sliced or cubed; ½ packet **chicken** strips; ½ packet **coriander**.
2 Drizzle 3-4 tablespoons low-oil **dressing** over the whole salad and add a grinding of black pepper.
3 Drizzle the remaining avo with lemon juice and refrigerate.

Snack 1 **pear**, quartered, dipped into 4 rounded tablespoons (⅓ tub) **cottage cheese**.

Chickpea, coriander and chicken salad.

TUESDAY

Breakfast FRUIT AND OATS

1 Heat ½ cup of **milk** in a cereal bowl or large mug.
2 Stir in 4 rounded tablespoons of **oats** and leave to soak while you eat the **fruit salad** or chunks.
3 Roughly chop 1 tablespoon of **nuts** and mix into the warm oats (with a teaspoon of sugar if desired).

Snack 1 **apple**, quartered, with ⅓ of the packet of **smoked salmon (trout)** or **beef** wrapped around each quarter.

Lunch SMOKED TROUT AND ROCKET SANDWICH

1 Halve ½ punnet of **cherry tomatoes** and place in a large mug. Drizzle with 1 tablespoon of salad **dressing** and microwave on high for 30 seconds.
2 Mash ¼ **avocado** and spread over a slice of **rye bread**. Top this with half the rocket.
3 Pile the warm tomatoes over the rocket.
4 Loosely pile the remaining **salmon**, **trout** or **beef** (from the snack) on top.

Snack A handful of **snap peas** with 3 **falafels**.

WEDNESDAY

Breakfast FRUIT AND AVO ON RYE

1 Toast 1 slice of **rye bread** and spread with 1 tablespoon of **relish**, **preserve** or **sweet-chilli sauce**.
2 Slice the remaining ¼ **avocado** onto the bread.
3 Top with 4 rounded tablespoons (⅓ of the tub) **cottage cheese**.
4 Thinly slice 1 **pear** on top of the cottage cheese. Season with **black pepper**.

Snack A handful of **grapes** (about 100 g) or a **banana** with 3 **falafels**.

Lunch FINGER LUNCH

1 Place the following on a dinner plate: ½ punnet of **cherry tomatoes**; ½ packet of **baby carrots** and ½ of the midi **cucumber**, quartered lengthwise.
2 Open the fruit **yoghurt** and use as the dip for the crudités.
3 Slice ¼ of the round or wedge of **cheese** onto 4 **Provitas** and enjoy with the crudités and dip.

Snack 1 **apple**, quartered, and dipped into the remaining ⅓ tub of **cottage cheese**.

THURSDAY

Breakfast CHICKEN ON RYE

1 Mash the last ¼ **avocado** onto a slice of **rye bread**.
2 Top with the remaining ½ packet of **chicken strips** and season with black pepper and salt, if needed.
3 Enjoy with 1 **pear**.

Snack 1 **banana** or a handful (100 g) of **grapes** with 1 tablespoon of **nuts**.

Lunch TUNA AND CHICKPEA SALAD

1 In a bowl make the salad by mixing: $1/3$ tin of drained **chickpeas**; 1 sachet of **tuna**; ½ packet **baby carrots**, sliced; ½ tub **beetroot**, quartered; 1 **apple**, chopped; the remaining **rocket** and 1-2 tablespoons low-oil **dressing**.

Snack 1 small **snack bar** (500 kJ; 6 g fat)

FRIDAY

Breakfast FRUITY OATS IN A MUG

1 Heat ½ cup of **milk** in a large mug. Stir in 4 rounded tablespoons of **oats** and leave to soak for 2 minutes.
2 Slice 1 **banana** or a handful (100 g) of **grapes** and mix into the oats.
3 Roughly chop 1 tablespoon of **nuts** and mix into the warm oats (with a teaspoon of sugar if desired).

Snack 1 **pear** with the remaining quarter round or wedge of **cheese**.

Lunch FALAFELS WITH CHOPPED SALAD

1 In a bowl combine: ½ punnet of **cherry tomatoes**, quartered; ½ midi **cucumber**, cubed; the rest of the **coriander** leaves, roughly chopped with the tub of **Greek yoghurt**.
2 Top the salad with 6 **falafels**.

Snack 1 **banana** or a handful (100 g) of **grapes** with 1 tablespoon of **nuts**.

BASKET TWO

FRUIT AND VEGETABLES

Baby carrots, 1 x small packet (100 g)
Carrot and pineapple salad, 250 g
Cherry tomatoes, 1 x small punnet
Coriander or basil, 1 x small packet (30 g)
Cranberries, dried, 1 x small packet (100 g)
Crudités packs (cheese, cucumber, carrot, olives), 2 x small packs
    (100 g each)
Grapes, 1 x punnet (300 g)
Mixed lettuce, 1 x bag (100 g)
Papinos, 3 small
Pears, pack of 4
Rosa tomato green salad, 1 tub (up to 200 g)
Snap peas, 1 x small packet (100 g)
Sprouts, 1 x tray (smallest available)
Sun-dried tomatoes in vinegar, 1 x stand-up pouch (240 g)

STARCHES

Men: You have the option of doubling the starch or the protein in your
    meals. If you choose to double the starch, then choose the amounts
    in **bold** below.

Four-bean salad, 1 x tub (250 g) **(not to be doubled, use an extra slice of
                                        bread or 4 Provitas)**
Microwave popcorn*, plain salted, 1 x packet (100 g)
Oats, 1 x box (500 g or smaller)
Provitas or rye bread, 1 x box with individual packs of 4 Provitas or
    1 x packet bread (8 slices)
Sweetcorn, 1 x tin (410 g)   **(2 x tins)**

*   *Popcorn must be plain salted as the fat content is already 13 g per
    100 g which means half the packet (one snack) contains just over the
    recommended 6 g of fat. Do not choose a flavoured popcorn such as
    buttered as it would contain at least double the fat.*

PROTEIN AND DAIRY

Men: You have the option of doubling the starch or the protein in your meals. If you choose to double the protein, choose the amounts in **bold** below.

Eggs, hard boiled on Sunday night, x 2 **(4 x eggs)**

Fish cakes, 1 x pack of 4 (300 g) **(not to be doubled, use 50% more at meals = 6 fish cakes = 400 g)**

Low-fat fruit smoothie, 1 x bottle (300 ml)

Milk, low fat, 1% or skimmed, 1 L

Mini cheese portion*, preferably lower fat, 1 x single serve (25-30 g each) **(2 x single serves)**

Smoked chicken breasts, 1 x pack of 2 small breasts (maximum 250 g) **(4 small breasts – max 500 g)**

Tzatziki dip, 1 x mini tub (about 100 g)

Yoghurt, fruit, low fat, 3 x small tubs (100-150 ml)

* *If the crudités do not include cheese, buy two extra cheese portions.*

FATS

Low-oil mayonnaise, 1 x small bottle

Low-oil salad dressing, 1 x small bottle

Sunflower or pumpkin seeds, 1 x small packet (100 g)

EXTRAS

Lemon juice, 1 x small bottle

OPTIONAL EXTRAS (can be added to any meal)

Artichokes in brine

Asparagus spears

Fresh herbs

Gherkins

Mushrooms in brine

Peppadews

Pickled onions

Sprouts

Vinegar, balsamic or other

MONDAY

Breakfast FISH CAKE AND SUN-DRIED TOMATO

1. Break up 1 **fish cake** onto 4 **Provitas** or 1 slice of **rye bread**.
2. Place ¼ of the **sun-dried tomatoes** in vinegar on top of the fish cake.
3. Serve with 1 **papino**, halved and depipped.

Snack A handful (100 g) of **grapes** mixed into 1 small tub of **fruit yoghurt**, in a bowl or mug.

Lunch SMOKED CHICKEN WITH CARROT AND PINEAPPLE SALAD

1. Mix ⅓ of the packet of **sprouts** into the **carrot and pineapple salad**.
2. Serve with 4 **Provitas** or 1 slice of **rye bread** topped with 1 sliced **smoked chicken breast** and drizzled with 2 tablespoons of **low-oil mayonnaise**.

Snack ½ packet of microwave **popcorn** (keep the other half for tomorrow's afternoon snack).

TUESDAY

Breakfast EGG AND SMOOTHIE

1. Slice 1 hard-boiled **egg** onto 2 **Provitas** or ½ slice of **rye bread** and eat with the bought fruit **smoothie**. Keep the left-over bread for your mid-morning snack.

Snack Place the cheese from 1 **crudités** pack on 2 **Provitas** or ½ slice of **rye bread** and enjoy with the rest of the crudités pack.

Lunch SWEETCORN SALAD WITH FISH CAKE

1. Place ¼ of the packet of **lettuce** leaves on a dinner plate and top with 1 **fish cake**.
2. Serve with a salad made from ½ tin drained **sweetcorn**; ¼ of the **sun-dried tomatoes**; ⅓ of the packet of **sprouts**; ½ packet of **coriander** or **basil** and 1-2 tablespoons of low-oil **dressing** or **mayonnaise**.

Snack ½ packet of microwave **popcorn** (from yesterday).

WEDNESDAY

Breakfast FRUIT SALAD AND YOGHURT

1. Prepare a fruit salad using 1 small **papino**; 1 **pear**; a handful (100 g) of **grapes** and 2-4 teaspoons lemon juice.
2. Serve half of this fruit salad with 1 tub of fruit **yoghurt** topped with 2 tablespoons **sunflower** or **pumpkin seeds**. Keep the other half of the fruit salad for your mid-morning snack.

Snack The other half of the **fruit salad** sprinkled with 1 tablespoon **sunflower** or **pumpkin seeds**.

Lunch FOUR-BEAN SALAD

1. Make a large salad using the tub of **Rosa tomato green salad**; the tub of **four-bean salad** and ½ packet of **coriander** or **basil**.

Snack 4 **Provitas** or 1 slice of **rye bread** with 1 mini single serve **cheese** portion.

THURSDAY

Breakfast SWISS MUESLI

1. Soak 4 rounded tablespoons of **oats** in ½ cup of **milk** for about 10 minutes.
2. Grate or finely chop 1 fresh **pear** and mix into the oats together with 2 tablespoons dried **cranberries**.

Snack 1 **papino** drizzled with lemon juice.

Lunch SMOKED CHICKEN SALAD

1. Make a layered salad in a bowl using ¼ packet **lettuce** leaves, ½ tin drained **sweetcorn**, 1 sliced smoked **chicken breast**, ½ punnet halved **cherry tomatoes**, ⅓ packet of **sprouts** and ¼ of the **sun-dried tomatoes** in vinegar.
2. Drizzle with 3-4 teaspoons low-oil salad **dressing** or **mayonnaise**.

Snack ½ packet of dried **cranberries** with 2 tablespoons **sunflower** or **pumpkin seeds**.

FRIDAY

Breakfast EGG ON CRACKERS
(pictured)

1. Halve a handful (100 g) of **grapes** into a large mug and pour a tub of fruit **yoghurt** over the grapes, or eat separately.
2. Serve with 1 sliced hard-boiled **egg** on 4 **Provitas** or 1 slice of **rye bread** drizzled with 2 tablespoons low-oil **dressing** or **mayonnaise** and the last of the **sun-dried tomatoes** in vinegar.

Snack Place the cheese from 1 **crudités** pack on 2 **Provitas** or ½ slice of **rye bread** and enjoy with the rest of the crudités pack.

Lunch FISH CAKES WITH CRUDITÉS AND TZATZIKI DIP

1. Place 1 mini tub **tzatziki** onto the middle of a plate.
2. Place the remaining 2 **fish cakes** on one side of the tzatziki and 1 small packet **baby carrots**, 1 small packet **snap peas** and ½ punnet of **cherry tomatoes** on the other side of the tzatziki.
3. Dip the fish cakes and crudités into the tzatziki and enjoy your finger lunch.

Snack 1 **pear** with the rest of the dried **cranberries** and **sunflower** or **pumpkin seeds**.

Egg on crackers.

BASKET THREE

FRUIT AND VEGETABLES

Apples, tray of 4
Baby cucumbers, courgette size, 1 small packet
Bananas (small), packet of 4
Cherry tomatoes, 1 small punnet
Fresh berries of choice, 1 small punnet
Fresh fruit chunks tub, 2 x 150 g tubs
Fruit flakes or dainties, 1 pouch with 5 x 40 g mini packets
Mixed crudités (carrots, cucumber, tomatoes, celery), 1 x 350 g tray
Mixed lettuce, 1 x 100 g packet
Tomato, fresh, 1 large
Yellow pepper, 1 pepper

STARCHES

Men: You have the option of doubling the starch or the protein in your meals. If you choose to double the starch, then the packet sizes below will be enough.

Instant oats, original flavour only or low-GI muesli sachets, 2 sachets
Mini pitas, 1 x packet of 12
Provitas (optional), 1 box containing individual packs of 4
Rye bread, wheat free, sliced, 1 packet

PROTEIN AND DAIRY

Men: You have the option of doubling the starch or the protein in your meals. If you choose to double the protein, then choose the amounts in **bold** below.

Danish herring, chopped, 1 x 250 g tub or
    smoked salmon, 1 x 100 g packet   **(2 tubs or 200 g salmon)**
Eggs, hard boiled on Sunday night, x 2   **(4 x eggs)**
Milk, low fat, 1% or skimmed, 1 L

Mini serve cheese portions, preferably
    lower fat, 2 x 25-30 g portions   **(4 mini portions)**
Shaved chicken, smoked or plain, 1 x 125 g packet **(2 x 125 g)**
Shaved ham, 1 x 125 g packet   **(2 x 125 g)**
Tzatziki, 1 x 200 g tub
Yoghurt, fruit, low fat, 6 x 100-150 ml

FATS

Almonds or pecans, 1 x 100 g packet
Hummus, reduced fat, 1 x 200 g tub
Low-fat mayonnaise, 1 x small bottle

EXTRAS

Low-oil salad dressing, 1 x small bottle
Sweet-chilli sauce, 1 x small bottle

OPTIONAL EXTRAS (can be added to any meal)

Artichokes in brine
Asparagus spears
Fresh herbs
Gherkins
Mushrooms in brine
Peppadews
Pickled onions
Sprouts
Vinegar, balsamic or other

MONDAY

Breakfast OATS AND BERRIES

1 Heat 175 ml (¾ cup) **milk** in a mug if using oats.
2 Empty 1 packet instant **oats** or **muesli** into a cereal bowl and mix in the milk.
3 Add ½ punnet of **berries** and 5 chopped **nuts** and mix into the oat porridge or muesli.
4 Sweeten with 1 teaspoon sugar if desired.

Snack 1 tub of **fresh fruit chunks**.

Lunch HERRING SALAD IN MINI PITAS

1 Make a salad using ¼ packet of **lettuce** – keeping the larger leaves for Friday – ½ packet of **mixed crudités** and ½ tub of **Danish herring** (or ½ the **smoked salmon**).
2 Slice open 3 **mini pitas** and drizzle 1 teaspoon of **sweet-chilli sauce** into each pita.
3 Overfill each pita with the fish salad.

Snack 1 low-fat fruit **yoghurt** and 10 **nuts**.

TUESDAY

Breakfast FRUIT WITH EGG ON RYE

1 Enjoy 1 tub of **fresh fruit chunks**.
2 Warm the **rye bread** or 2 **mini pitas** briefly in a toaster, and slice the hard-boiled **egg** on top of the bread or into the pitas. Drizzle with 1 tablespoon low-oil **mayonnaise**.

Snack 1 **apple** and 1 small **banana**.

Lunch FINGER LUNCH WITH BERRY YOGHURT DESSERT

1 Pile ½ packet **shaved chicken** onto 4 **Provitas** or 1 slice of **rye bread**.
2 Dip ½ the tray of **mixed crudités** into ½ tub of **hummus**.
3 Finish off with ½ punnet of **berries** mixed into 1 tub of **yoghurt**.

Snack 1 x 40 g packet of **fruit flakes** or **dainties** with 10 **nuts**.

WEDNESDAY

Breakfast BANANA OATS

1 Heat 175 ml (¾ cup) **milk** in a mug if using oats.
2 Empty 1 packet instant **oats** or **muesli** into a cereal bowl and mix in the milk.
3 Slice 1 **banana** into the oat porridge or muesli.
4 Sweeten with 1 teaspoon sugar if desired.

Snack 1 **apple** with a mini **cheese** portion.

Lunch SALSA WITH HAM-FILLED PITAS

1 Make the salsa by finely chopping the ½ punnet **cherry tomatoes** and 2 mini **cucumbers** and mixing with 4 tablespoons of **low-oil dressing**.
2 Shred ¼ packet of **lettuce**, keeping the larger leaves for Friday.
3 Slice open 3 **mini pitas** and fill generously with the shredded lettuce and ½ packet of **shaved ham**.
4 Finish off with 1 mini packet of **fruit flakes** or **dainties** as dessert.

Snack 1 low-fat fruit **yoghurt** and 10 **nuts**.

THURSDAY

Breakfast EGG MAYO

1 Mix 1 chopped **apple** and a tub of **yoghurt** in a bowl or mug.
2 Mash 1 hard-boiled **egg** with a tablespoon of **low-oil mayonnaise** and fill 2 **mini pitas**.

Snack 4 baby **cucumbers**, cut lengthwise with ½ tub of **hummus** as a dip.

Lunch OPEN HERRING SANDWICH WITH SALAD

1 Mix ½ punnet of halved **cherry tomatoes**, 1 sliced baby **cucumber**, ½ chopped **yellow pepper** and ¼ packet of **lettuce**, shredded, keeping the larger leaves for Friday.
2 Add and mix with ½ tub **tzatziki**.
3 Pile the remaining **Danish herring** or **smoked salmon** onto a slice of **rye bread** and enjoy with the salad.

Snack 1 small **banana** and 1 tub of **yoghurt**.

FRIDAY

Breakfast GRILLED TOMATO, (BANANA,) HAM AND CHEESE

1 Layer the sliced **tomato**, leftover **shaved ham** (and **banana**) on 1 slice of **rye bread**.
2 Thinly slice the **cheese** on top and microwave for a few seconds to melt the cheese.
3 The banana can be eaten separately, if preferred.

Snack 1 low-fat fruit **yoghurt** and 10 **nuts**.

Lunch LETTUCE AND CHICKEN WRAPS

(pictured)
1 Make a dipping sauce by mixing the leftover **tzatziki** with 4 teaspoons **sweet-chilli sauce** and 2 teaspoons water.
2 Using the large **lettuce** leaves, make lettuce wraps by layering lettuce and the remaining **shaved chicken** (65 g).
3 Slice ½ **yellow pepper** and 2 **mini cucumbers** lengthwise and place over the chicken and lettuce.
4 Roll up the lettuce leaves to make wraps and dip into the dipping sauce.
5 Enjoy the **apple** as dessert.
6 Optional: Add 3-4 Provitas or 1 slice of bread.

Snack 1 x 40 g packet of **fruit flakes** or **dainties** with 10 **nuts**.

Lettuce and chicken wraps.

APPENDIX

CHECKLISTS FOR MEALS AND SNACKS

These checklists are ideal for you to copy, cut out and laminate. Keep them in your handbag, car, briefcase, wallet or back pocket for easy reference.

Snacks for women
- ☐ 500 kJ (120 calories)
- ☐ Less than 25 g carbohydrate
- ☐ 5-10 g fat
- ☐ More than 2 g fibre
- ☐ Lower GI

Snacks for men
- ☐ 750 kJ (180 calories)
- ☐ 35 g carbohydrate
- ☐ 5-10 g fat
- ☐ More than 2 g fibre
- ☐ Lower GI

Meals for women
- ☐ 1 500-1 800 kJ
- ☐ 10-15 g fat
- ☐ Less than 45 g carbohydrate
- ☐ Less than 25 g protein
- ☐ More than 5 g fibre
- ☐ Colour from vegetables, salad or fruit

Meals for men
- ☐ 1 800-2 200 kJ
- ☐ 10-15 g fat
- ☐ Less than 60 g carbohydrate
- ☐ About 25 g protein
- ☐ More than 5 g fibre
- ☐ Colour from vegetables, salad or fruit

Smoothies and meals in a glass for women
- ☐ 1 200-1 800 kJ
- ☐ 5-15 g fat
- ☐ Less than 50 g carbohydrate
- ☐ Protein : carbohydrate at least 1 : 2
- ☐ Preferably some fibre

Smoothies and meals in a glass for men
- ☐ 1 500-2 000 kJ
- ☐ 5-15 g fat
- ☐ Less than 60 g carbohydrate
- ☐ Protein : carbohydrate at least 1 : 2
- ☐ Preferably some fibre

Bran muffin, ginger biscuits and almond biscotti.
(Recipes on pages 184, 186 and 187.)

QUICK AND EASY RECIPES

BRAN MUFFINS
[Taken from the low-GI recipe book: *Eating for Sustained Energy 1* by Liesbet Delport and Gabi Steenkamp (Registered Dieticians), Tafelberg (2006).]

Makes 24 large muffins or 48 mini muffins

NOTE: This batter has to stand overnight or for at least 2 hours.

2 eggs
1 c soft brown sugar (250 ml)
4 T canola oil (60 ml)
2 c low-fat milk (500 ml)
1 t vanilla essence (5 ml)
1 c oat bran (250 ml)
1½ c flour (375 ml)
2 c digestive bran (500 ml)
½ t salt (2 ml)
3 t bicarbonate of soda (15 ml)
1 t cinnamon (5 ml)
1 large apple, grated
1 c sultanas (250 ml)

1   In a very large bowl beat together the eggs, sugar and oil.
2   Add the milk and vanilla to the egg mixture.
3   Add all the dry ingredients, grated apple and the sultanas.
4   Stir with a wooden spoon until well blended.
5   Cover and leave in the fridge overnight or for at least 2 hours.
6   When ready to bake, stir and drop into lightly greased muffin pans (fill ¾ full).
7   Bake at 180 °C for 15 minutes.

This mixture can be kept in the fridge for up to 30 days. Do not freeze the batter.
Baked muffins freeze very well. These muffins are deliciously moist and do not need to be spread with margarine or butter.

Nutrients per muffin
GI lower (58)
Fat 3 g
Carbohydrate 22 g
Fibre 3 g
Protein 3 g
kJ 550
GL 13

One muffin is equivalent to 1 starch, 1 fruit and ½ fat.

LEGAL CHEESE SAUCE FOR VEGETABLES

[Taken from the low-GI recipe book: *Eating for Sustained Energy 1* by Liesbet Delport and Gabi Steenkamp (Registered Dieticians), Tafelberg (2006).]

Serves 6

2 t lite margarine (10 ml)
$^3/_5$ c low-fat milk (150 ml)
$^3/_5$ c water from boiling or micro-waving vegetables* (150 ml)
¼ t salt (1 ml)
½ t mustard powder (3 ml)
3 T flour (45 ml)
60 g (2 matchboxes) lower fat Cheddar cheese, grated
½ t Parmesan cheese, grated (3 ml) (optional)

1 Melt the margarine over low heat. Add the milk and vegetable water, then add the salt and mustard powder. Bring to the boil.
2 Meanwhile mix the flour to a smooth paste with a little water.
3 As soon as the milk boils, pour a little hot milk onto the flour mixture and stir well. Pour the flour and water mixture back onto the rest of the boiled milk and vegetable water.
4 Return to the heat and boil until the sauce thickens.
5 Add the grated cheeses and pour over cooked vegetables.

Broccoli, cauliflower and cour-gettes (baby marrow) make the tastiest vegetable water for cheese sauce. If vegetable water is not available, use 10 ml stock powder and 150 ml boiling water.

Boxed long-life milk gives a creamier sauce without adding any extra fat. Parmesan cheese is high in fat but very strong in flavour. By adding just half a teaspoon to a dish with cheese, one is able to use less than half the amount of cheese – and half the fat – without sacrificing flavour. For a plain white sauce, omit the cheeses and add a dash of nutmeg.

Nutrients per serving of 4 T (60 ml)
GI low (55)
Fat 5 g
Carbohydrate 5 g
Fibre negligible
Protein 4 g
kJ 322
GL 2

One serving is equivalent to ½ dairy and ½ fat.

GINGER BISCUITS
Makes about 100 biscuits

2 c cake flour (500 ml)
4 t ground ginger (20 ml)
1 c whole-wheat Pronutro (250 ml)
1 c oat bran (250 ml)
1½ c sugar (375 ml)
2 t bicarbonate of soda (10 ml)
2 t fat-free milk (10 ml)
½ c low-GI apricot jam (125 ml)
1 egg
1 small apple, peeled and grated
1 c butter (250 ml)

1   Preheat the oven to 180 °C and spray one or more baking sheets with non-stick cooking spray.
2   Sift the flour and ginger into a large bowl. Add the whole-wheat Pronutro, oat bran and sugar.
3   In a separate bowl, mix the bicarbonate of soda with the milk and add the apricot jam. While it foams stir until smooth to ensure that there are no lumps left in the jam.
4   Beat the egg and add this, as well as the grated apple to the bicarbonate of soda, milk and apricot jam mixture.
5   Rub the butter into the dry ingredients.
6   Add the jam mixture to the dry ingredients and form a soft dough, using a fork or spoon. The mixture is crumbly, but persevere.
7   Spoon teaspoonfuls onto the baking sheet(s), 5 cm apart, using two teaspoons, to yield 100 biscuits. Flatten slightly using the teaspoons and bake for 10-15 minutes per batch until brown.
8   Remove the biscuits from the oven and cool slightly before removing from the baking tray.
9   Cool completely before storing in an airtight container.

If using a convection oven, more than one baking sheet with biscuits can be baked at a time.

Even though these biscuits are lower GI and lower fat, fruit should still be the preferred snack, as it contains more fibre and micronutrients, and is also fat free. Butter is used in these biscuits to make them crisper, as oat bran and especially apples in biscuits are inclined to make them soft. Although butter is high in saturated fat, we controlled the amount used in this recipe so that each biscuit contains about 1 g saturated fat.
Remember that these biscuits are not a free food! A maximum of two biscuits is the recommended portion for a snack.

Nutrients per biscuit

GI intermediate (61)

Fat 2.1 g

Saturated fat 1.1 g

Carbohydrate 7 g

Fibre 0.5 g

Protein 0.6 g

kJ 207

GL 4

One biscuit is equivalent to ½ starch plus ½ fat.

ALMOND BISCOTTI/RUSKS
Makes 25 biscotti

3 extra-large eggs

½ c sugar (125 ml)

1 t almond essence (5 ml)

½ t vanilla essence (2.5 ml)

1 c cake flour (250 ml)

2 t baking powder (10 ml)

¼ t salt (1 ml)

¼ t ground nutmeg (1 ml)

2 c whole-wheat Pronutro, original (250 ml)

1 c oat bran (250 ml)

2-4 T cake flour (30-60 ml) for kneading the dough

½ packet flaked almonds or almond nibs (50 g)

1   Preheat the oven to 180 °C and lightly grease a baking sheet with non-stick cooking spray, unless you choose to use a silicone baking sheet which does not require greasing.

2   In a large bowl, whisk together the eggs, sugar, almond and vanilla essence until light and creamy – about 5 minutes.

3   Sift the flour, baking powder, salt and nutmeg on top and beat into the egg mixture.

4   Add the Pronutro and mix to form a soft, crumbly dough.

5 Add the oat bran and, using a wooden spoon, mix into the dough.

6 Sprinkle 2 tablespoons of flour onto a clean work surface and sprinkle the flaked almonds on top of the flour.

7 Place the dough on the almonds. Dust your hands with a table-spoon of flour and then gather up the dough with your hands and work into a smooth ball, incorporating all the almonds. Flour your hands again if the dough sticks to them.

8 When all the almonds have been incorporated, divide into 2 "logs", each about 30 cm long and 5 cm wide. Place the logs side by side at least 6 cm apart on the lightly greased baking sheet. Flatten each log slightly with the palm of your hand.

9 Bake in the preheated oven for 30 minutes until deep cream in colour.

10 Remove from the oven and reduce the oven temperature to 120 °C. Leave to cool for 5 minutes.

11 Place each log onto a breadboard and carefully cut diagonally into 25 x 1 cm slices. Place the slices flat on the baking sheet and bake for another 60 minutes until they are dry and just beginning to look toasted.

12 Turn the oven off and leave the biscotti to cool in the cooling oven.

13 Store in an airtight container for up to 2 months. One biscotti makes an ideal snack serving.

The fat in these delicious biscotti is from the almonds and the egg yolks, which are both good sources of the more beneficial mono-unsaturated fats.

Nutrients per biscotti
GI intermediate (61)
Fat 2.4 g
Saturated fat 0.4 g
Carbohydrate 14 g
Fibre 2.2 g
Protein 3 g
kJ 376
GL 8

One serving of 1 biscotti is equivalent to 1 starch plus ½ fat.

INDEX